ABOUT THE AUTHOR

James Wren was born in 1825, but ̶ ̶ ̶ ̶ ̶ known
of his early life. He did start ̶ ̶ ̶ ̶ ̶ ̶ it of a
machine company in Po̶ ̶ ̶ ̶ ̶ ̶ ̶
company to which h̶ ̶ ̶ ̶ ̶ ̶ ̶ 863
when he resigned his ̶e
army, he married twi̶ ̶ ̶ ̶ ̶ ̶ ̶ ̶ ̶ ̶ ̶ ̶ ̶ ̶ by both
wives. Wren's personal ̶ ̶ ̶ ̶ ̶ ̶ ̶ ̶ ̶ed to obscurity
after the Civil War end̶ ̶ ̶ ̶ ̶ ̶ ̶amily's history recorded
him as living in Boyertown, Pennsylvania, in 1907,
which would have made him eighty-two years old at
that time.

ABOUT THE EDITOR IN CHIEF

John Michael Priest is the author of the highly ac-
claimed *Antietam: The Soldiers' Battle* and the forthcoming history of the Battle of South Mountain. He is a
graduate of Loyola College, Baltimore, Maryland, and
teaches at South Hagerstown High School, where he
developed the idea for this book with his students.
Priest resides with his family in Boonsboro, Maryland,
near the battlefields he studies.

PRAISE FOR
JOHN MICHAEL PRIEST'S ANTIETAM

"Here is a book that reaches deep into scattered manuscript sources to provide a service for the men who
fought at Antietam."

—Jay Luvaas,
U.S. Army Military History Institute

"A book that every student of the Eastern theater
should have."

—*Richmond News-Leader*

CAPTAIN JAMES WREN'S CIVIL WAR DIARY

From New Bern to Fredericksburg

B Company, 48th Pennsylvania Volunteers
February 20, 1862 – December 17, 1862

John Michael Priest
Editor in Chief

Robert Brown
Assistant Editor

Brian Blickenstaff   Jessica Rauth
Peter Cartwright   Christopher Shank
Jennifer Groves   Marla Shetron
Robert Mueller   Jessica Sprecher
Matthew Pfister   Stephen Wyatt

Research Assistants

South Hagerstown High School
Maryland

B

BERKLEY BOOKS, NEW YORK

This project was made possible through a grant from
the Maryland Humanities Council and the National
Endowment for the Humanities.

This Berkley book contains the complete text of the original hard-
cover edition. It has been completely reset in a typeface designed
for easy reading and was printed from new film.

CAPTAIN JAMES WREN'S CIVIL WAR DIARY:
FROM NEW BERN TO FREDERICKSBURG

A Berkley Book / published by arrangement with
White Mane Publishing Company, Inc.

PRINTING HISTORY
White Mane Publishing edition published 1990
Berkley trade paperback edition / November 1991

ISBN: 0-425-13034-7

A BERKLEY BOOK ® TM 757,375
Berkley Books are published by The Berkley Publishing Group,
200 Madison Avenue, New York, New York 10016.
The name "Berkley" and the "B" logo
are trademarks belonging to Berkley Publishing Corporation.

PRINTED IN THE UNITED STATES OF AMERICA
10   9   8   7   6   5   4   3   2   1

Acknowledgments

For the past several years, while doing research on *Antietam: The Soldiers' Battle*, I have been using excerpts from James Wren's diary to illustrate in the classroom what I consider to be one of the most interesting Civil War diaries I have ever read. This year, I decided to involve the students in research at a major research facility to introduce them to the work of the historian. The results are before you now.

We wish to thank Dr. Richard Sommers, and Mr. Michael Winey of the United States Army Military History Institute at Carlisle Barracks, Pennsylvania, and their staffs, who made their manuscript and photo collections available to us. It was an experience which my students will long remember with a certain amount of awe.

I also want to thank Lieutenant Colonel Andreson, Deputy Director of the United States Military History Institute, for his cooperation in facilitating our field trip to Carlisle Barracks.

As always, not enough can be said about Antietam National Battlefield's Superintendent Richard Rambur and his staff, Ed Mazzer, Paul Chiles, and Ted Alexander for allowing us to copy the typescript diary which is in their collection. They are a pleasure to work with and have "bent over backwards" to assist us in gathering information.

A hearty "thank you" goes to Robert Brown, TAG Office, Board of Education of Washington County, Maryland. It was a real relief to have him fill out the grant forms to The Maryland Humanities Council. More importantly, he compiled a complete roster of individuals for the students to identify. His enthusiasm in the project was most refreshing.

The Maryland Humanities Council and the National En-

v

dowment for the Humanities funded the original project. Without their monies we could never have started it at all.

My special regards, however, have to be reserved for the ten students who did the ground work for the diary.

Rob Mueller transcribed the Pollock letters. I loved his particular insights about the young lieutenant, which generally ran along the lines of, "Mr. Priest, he's always crying home to Ma or Pa."

Matt Pfister drew two of the maps, produced a line drawing of James Wren, and worked on the regimental rosters with great attention to detail.

Jessica Sprecher and Marla Shetron worked as a team collecting copies of the generals' service records and collecting Bosbyshell's and Gould's accounts of the 48th Pennsylvania.

Jessica Rauth did excellent work collecting service records of obscure individuals, in particular, Lieutenant Daniel Flagler.

Jennifer Groves took the photographs used in the manuscript: she also assisted in gathering information from the *Official Records*, which we used to verify other accounts of the regiment.

Chris Shank spent several Sunday afternoons at my house typing the manuscript and working in the Western Maryland Room at the Washington County Free Library; he also worked with the *Official Records*.

Brian Blickenstaff did a very good job transcribing anecdotes from Wren's papers for use in the book. He made some rather astute observations about Wren, in particular, the captain's ability to capture a man's dialect on paper.

Pete Cartwright not only worked on the rosters but he also did transcription work in the manuscript department. I will never forget how the vastness of the Military History Institute's holdings amazed him. He thoroughly enjoyed working with the original documents.

Steve Wyatt did a lot of the drudgery work. He spent quite a few Sunday hours at my home typing the edited manuscript. He was always willing to volunteer when he could find the time. I appreciate his cooperation.

This book is a testimony to what students can and will do given the opportunity. These pupils are among the best I have had the pleasure of working with.

Many thanks go to Dr. Rick Sauers (Harrisburg, PA) and Leo L. Ward, President of the Historical Society of Schuylkill County, for James Wren's biography.

I will never be able to adequately express my gratitude to White Mane Publishing of Shippensburg, Pennsylvania. Harold Collier, Duane Collier, and Dr. Martin Gordon, for financing the publication of the diary, are laying the ground work for future such projects. They sought me out to publish this study before I had a chance to introduce the concept to them. We are forever indebted to them.

Foreword

A quick reading of the excerpt below illustrates the problems which we confronted in trying to put James Wren's colorful diary into readable English.

"September 17th 1862 Battle of Anttetan Bridg at ½ past 6 oclok A.M. our division was ordred to take the advance & oppend a reguler engagement under Command of Genl Stergi whou acted splendid in handling his troops we drove the eneymey from thear entrechmts & Baricades after 3 hours of heavy Musketry engagment the Reigments engagd at the entrence of the Bridg was the 2nd Meryland 6th Newhamshier & 9th Newhamshier 48th Pensylvania & 51st Pensylvania it was a Desperat strugle whough should have Controale of the bridg my Compny as Liing down in frunt of the entrence & firing diret into the rebil Barracades at the Butment of the Bridg & during the strugle one of the 6th newhamshir men Came to me & said he had got his finger shot off but he did not want to go to the rear and he had about 40 rounds of Cartridg in his Cartridge Box then i said well its victorey or deth hear thear is no moving or Commanding to be done hear as all the troops was working and firing into the Bridg & its Baricades. . . ."

The first thing we tried to determine was whether there was any consistency in his mispellings. There were few. He tended to leave the silent "e" off words and he generally omitted double consonants. I tried to correct these in the original editing of the manuscript.

Wren also spelled phonetically. Words like "general" and "regiment" he usually copied as "genrel" and "reigment". We tried to keep as many of these words as they were in the original text.

The rhyme "i" before "e", except after "c" eluded the captain entirely. He consistently penned the words "received" and "Lieutenant" in a variety of novel ways, which we altered to the correct spellings or abbreviations.

We altered words which Captain Wren usually wrote in two syllables instead of one to be consistent with the way he most often spelled them. "Coald" instead of "cold" and "Roale" in the place of "roll" are examples.

I capitalized the first word of every sentence, and the proper names; this includes all first names and surnames. We changed most of the spellings to their generally acceptable correct forms.

We punctuated the entire manuscript, which was no mean task. I recall that he had about four periods in the entire work.

Bracketed words or names indicate omissions in the text and were inserted to clarify sentences. [?] indicates that the original transcript was blank and the item in the bracket is our assumption.

As the editor-in-chief, I typed the footnotes and inserted them in the text, labeled the photographs, and did most of the editing. The students identified the individuals and recorded their service records, located the pictures to be taken, transcribed the material used in the footnote annotations, constructed the bibliography, and drew two of the maps. This is *their* work more than it is mine.

I want to commend them for deciding to take all the royalties earned from this project (after we reimburse the Maryland Humanities Council) and returning them to a special fund in our school for use in future projects such as this.

They are a terrific group of young men and women. I think the world of them. They have been a blessing to me.

—John Michael Priest
South Hagerstown High School, Maryland
May 1989

Contents

CAPTAIN JAMES WREN'S CIVIL WAR DIARY

1

The North Carolina Expedition:
February 20–July 7, 1862

Thursday, Febuary [February] 20th, 1862
Camp Windfield [Winfield][1]

This is one of the finest days we have had on Hatteras Island, and immediately after Breakfast the teams for our Transportation arrived at Fort Clark. We broke up housekeeping and sent our things up to Camp Windfield, [2nd] Lieut. [John L.] Wood [B Co.] accompanying the teams.[2] At ½ past 8 o'clock, [at] Fort Clark, of which I had the command of said post up to the time of leaving, I was relieved of my Command by [1st] Lieut. [Charles H.] Pope of [Btty. F] the 4th R. I. Battry [Battery] By order of Gen'l. [Thomas] Williams, which was complied with by turning over all the standing orders to my suckesser [sucessor] in [the] Command.[3] The ammunition in the magazen [magazine] was all [illegible] to [the] Lieut. Commanding [the] Post. We proceeded to Camp Windfield, and arrived in Camp at one o'clock P.M. I reported to Gen'l. Williams & he was very pleasant to us on our arrival and informed me to report to Col. [James] Nagle [48th PA] & he would assign me quarters.[4] After reporting to Col. Nagle, he assigned us a position

1

to pitch our tents as the barracks was not finished. It was not as Comfortable as it was in Fort Clark Barracks but it was only for a few days when we would be quartered in Barracks.

Friday, Feb. 21st, 1862
Camp Windfield

Weather very pleasant all day. At 8 o'clock A.M., I took my Company out on drill to participate in a Brigaid [Brigade] drill and the men was a little strange on account of being detached from the Regt. [regiment] so long, however, they done very well. The movements made by the Briggad [Brigade] were in the order of combat. Had Regimental drill in the afternoon after which a Company drill Combined with the Regimental Drill made three hours drill, which made it rather tiresome. Had dress peraid [parade] in the evening.

Saturday, Feb. 22nd, 1862
Camp Windfield

This forenoon it rained Considerable and in the afternoon a heavy fog set in. Had no drills except dress perad [parade], commanded by Lieut. Col. [Joshua K.] Sigfried. [1st] Lieut. [Ulysses A.] Bast [B Co.] received notis [notice] of being detailed as officer of the Guard for Tomorrow.[5] A Steamer arrived this morning from Old Point Comfort, bringing a large Quantity of express. Our regimental instruments for our band also Came with the express.

Sunday, Febury [February] 23rd, 1862
Camp Windfield

The weather was very pleasent [pleasant] this morning, but turned into a Cold fog towards evening. Had the regular Sunday inspection. Thear [there] was no drilling today except dress perad. The Chaplin [chaplain] held service in frunt [front] [of] Co. G. Quarters. Capt. [George M.]

Southmayd [A Co.] and [1st] Lieut. [Samuel G.] Bailey [A Co.] of the 11th Conn. Regt. paid us a visit at our Quarters and we had quite a jolly time of it.[6]

Monday, Febury 24th, 1862
Camp Windfield

The weather was very unplesent during the night & being in the tents, no fire Could be applied to our Comfort. Lieut. Bast [B Co.] was relieved by [1st] Lieut. [Abiel H.] Jackson of Co. A.[7] At 10 o'clock, the Gen'l & Staff imbarked [embarked] on board of a vessel to accompany the expedition of Burnside, which will sail in the Course of a few days. The Steamer S. R. Spaulding arrived hear [here] from Roanoke. She will proceed to Old Point Comfort. We moved today into the Quarters that Col. Nagle formerly occupied with his field & Staff. I was officer of the day today.

Tuesday, Febury 25th, 1862
Camp Windfield

This morning I moved my men into The Barracks that staff used to occupy. Lieut Bast [B Co.] commanded the Company on regimental drill and owing to the negligence of the Sergeant Major [Charles Loeser], the men drilled with thear [their] Knapsacks on.[8] The mail left for the North today.

Wensday [Wednesday], Febury 26th, 1862
Camp Windfield

On account of the weather being very stormy and ocationaley [occasionally] raining, we had but one drill to-day and no dress perade [parade]. The Steamer Eastren [Eastern] State arrived at the inlet, bringing with her a large mail for our Reigment [regiment]. [1st] Lieut. [Isaac F.] Brannan [K Co.], who had gone to Fortress Monroe for the band instruments, returned with the same boat, he having, in the meanwhile, bin [been] at home at Cressona, Sch. County. [Schuylkill Co., PA][9]

Thursday, Febury 27th, 1862
Camp Windfield

We had but one perade this morning and no drill nor dress perade for the purpose of giving the men an oppertunity [opportunity] of Cleaning up thear Arms and accoutrements and Quarters for tomorrow's general inspection and Muster for pay. In the meanwhile, Lieut. Bast [B Co.] & myself occupied our time in answering the letters we received yesterday. It rained very hard all night but Break forth with a Clear sky this morning and remained Clear all day.

Friday, Febury 28th, 1862
Camp Windfield

This morning broak [broke] forth in splendor. Consequently, our inspection and Mustering took place at the time ordered—at 9 o'clock. A review proceded [preceded] the inspection, Col. Nagle being the Reviewing [officer], as well as the inspector and Mustring [mustering] officer. It was a grand sight to see the Col. ride down in front of the line all alone on his Cream Coulered [colored] Charger & then take his position by the Coulers all by himself. My men was all in good condition for the [illegible].

Saturday, March 1st, 1862
Camp Windfield

The weather was very fine, this morning however somewhat cold, a very thin Coat of ice having formed on the ponds around our Quarters, but was hardly perceptible towards evening. A hazy and misty Clouds overspread the sky and after dark [it] Commenced to rain. Had our usual morning perade and a very short Regimental drill after which the men war [were] given thear afternoon holiday to Clean up for sunday. Had dress perad at the usual hour. Today, twenty-two men, Commanded by [2nd] Lieut. Charles [H.] Miller of Co. H, was detailed to Guard the property of Fort Clark.[10]

Sunday, March 2nd, 1862
Camp Windfield

Rained all last night and this forenoon. The rest of the day Continued to be Cloudy and a more dreary day I have neaver [never] experienced since in the service and on account of the rain had no inspection but had dress perade at the usual time. Spent the entire day in Quarters reading papers. Capt. [Henry] Pleasants [C Co.] visited my Quarters but [left(?)] owing to Lieut. Wood [B Co.] & myself being out visiting Capt. Ballance's [daughters (?)].[11] A resident of the island visited us in our Quarters this evening and invited us to pay him a visit at his residence of which we expected [accepted].

Monday, March 3rd, 1862
Camp Windfield

Weather was very Pleasant but unusually warm this morning. Consequently, we had our regular Perad and Drill, however, after dinner it Commenced to rain and the afternoon drill was dispenced with but [we] held dress perade. Rained very hard in the evening. Col. Nagle detailed two men from each Company to go to Hatteras and assist in getting the express boxes on board the vessels.

Tuesday, March 4, 1862
Camp Windfield

The weather was very pleasant but owing to the Parade ground being overflowed by the tide we had no drill. After the morning perade, [I took] the men through the manual at the Quarters. In the afternoon we had a two hours Company drill. Lieut. Bast [B Co.] & myself had a Dispute regarding the extending of skirmishers and I extended the men and then referred to the tactics and he was convinced and saw that I was right.

Wensday [Wednesday],
March 5th, 1862
Camp Windfield

This morning the sky was overcast with heavy Clouds and [it] Commenced to rain during the forenoon drill. The Col. & Lieut. Col. & Adj. & surgeon [Charles T.] Reber have gone up the island so Major [Daniel] Nagle had Command of the regimental Drill in the forenoon [and] also in the afternoon, which, however, was rather short on account of the rain.[12] [2nd] Lieut. [Oliver C.] Bosbyshell acted as adj.[13] I was detailed as officer of the day for tomorrow. Lieut. Wood [B Co.] [was] not attending drill on account of [illegible].

Thursday, March 6th, 1862
Camp Windfield

Weather was very pleasant. I acted as officer of the day. Consequently, Lieut. Bast [B Co.] had command of the Company. In the afternoon on regimental Drill, the regiment practiced firing with ball Cartridge. The Col. had intended to fire in the forenoon but, on account of Co. G having no Cartridge Boxes, after Regimental Drill, Lieut. Bast Drilled the Company in the skirmish drill with beaugel [bugle] sounds. I blew the Calls myself.

Friday, March 7th, 1862
Camp Windfield

This morning it Commenced to rain and, soon after, the rain and the wind Commenced to blow like all fury, which blew the watter [water] on the perade ground to the depth of Several feet. Consequently, morning perade was dispensed with and all the Companies, with the exception of ours, had Company drills in thear barracks, our men's Barracks being in [a] separate apartment. Dress perade was also dispensed with. Lieut. Wood [B Co.] procured a darky named Joseph S. Gibbons and, as he was got on the island of Hatteras and he Came into our service on Friday, we Christened him Joseph Friday. [1st] Lieut. [Henry] James [F Co.] received a furlough from Col. Nagle and he at once proceded to Hatteras to imbark on the steamer going north.[14] Was expected to leave in a few hours for Old Point Comfort.

Saturday, March 8th, 1862
Camp Windfield

Very Cold but [the] sun [was] shining pleasant all day. Morning perad and Regimental Drill in the forenoon, after which thear was no drills, merely dress perade. In the afternoon, the men had thear usual holiday for the purpose of preparing for tomorrow's inspection. Four men ware reprimanded by the Col. in the presence of the Regiment for leaving the picket Guard without leave and leaving thear posts without being properly relieved. This morning a steamer left the inlet for Philadelphia taking with her Major Nagle, Lieut. James [F Co.] and several others.

Sunday, March 9th, 1862
Camp Windfield

Weather very pleasant all day. Had the regular Sunday inspection at 8 o'clock, after which Lieut. Wood [B Co.] and myself took a Carriage Ride up to the light house & took with us the 2 Miss Ballances. Wood's rigging Consisted of a two wheeled gig & the one with 4 wheels I had, but having seen many years, it did not hurt the spectators' eyes as we passed with the gloss of finish that it bore. Yet it was very healthy as thear was a free Circulation of air [it] having no top. The harness caused our trip to be free from anything like sudden Jars, as the harnesses were princably Composed of rope & at the act of Collisions in the mud holes, they generally expanded sufficient to Cause Considerable opening betwixt the Carriage and the annimel [animal], however, we safely reached the Light house & then arrived at the dwelling of Mr. Neal whear we took dinner & spent a Very pleasant time. On our return home we had quite a lively time as the Ladies was very lively & all Came off very well. Heard no complaint except that on wash day, I heard that thear was a scarcity of wash Lines and I guess it was accounted for in our harness as that was the principal quality of our outfit.

Monday, March 10th [1862]
Camp Windfield

Weather still pleasant in the forenoon but got to be cloudy in the afternoon and rained a little in the evening. Lieut. Bast [B Co.] went on duty as officer of the Guard. The mail that the steamer braught [brought] yesterday we received this forenoon but it was rather a small one, but 3 [letters] came of which Bast received one. Received letters informing us of the safe arrival of our men's moneys at home.

Tuesday, March 11, 1862
Camp Windfield

The guard had a very bad night last night, it raining nearly all night, making it very disagreeable. Lieut. Wood [B Co.] went as officer of the guard relieving Lieut. Bast [B Co.]. This morning at 7 o'clock, the steamer S. R. Spaulding arrived from Old Point Comfort bringing the paymaster with her. She also braught the news of a naval engagement at that place. Received orders to march with 5 days rashons [rations] and no Camp equipage but with 60 rounds of Cartridge. Wood was relieved again by [2nd] Lieut. Jacob Douty [K Co.].[15] All our men on duty war called in.

Wensday, March 12th, 1862
Hatteras Beach[16]

Relieved this morning at 4 o'clock. Had breakfast at 5, formed line at 6:40 [A.M.] and started at 7 o'clock from Camp Windfield. When leaving Camp, the remaining Companies gave nine hearty Cheers which was promptly responded to by the going Battalion. Arrived at Hatteras at 9 o'clock whear we found that the steamer George Peabody on which we ware to imbark was hard aground on the sand bar. War unable to get her off during the day. Consequently, we had to remain on the beach all day. The men by some means or other got Liquor and Consequently got drunk & they got fighting amongst themselves in Compny C, and fighting was the order of the day. Daniel Root of my Company got in a fight and I put him in the guard house until night.[17] Whearever we could find any [illegible] laid down in the sand in the open air, others in wagons that was on the beach. I quartered over at Fort Clark with Lieut. Miller [H Co.]. It had the appearance of rain towards night.

Thursday, March 13, 1862
George Peabody on Pamlico Sounds, N.C.

Slept Very little last night on account of the men who ware drunk bawling around the shelter like a lot of mad men. About 12 o'clock, Midnight, a lot of drunken men, mostly of Compny C, got into a building occupied by Conterbands [contrabands] and abused them most shamefully, using bayonets and Knives, Cutting severel [several] very severely. Old Gallaway, [the] Colnal's [colonel's] Coulered servent [servant], having bin in for the night, received a Cut in the stomach which will undoubtedly prove fatal.[18] A Contarband [contraband] had a finger Cut off, [and] the sinew of his left hand Cut. On arising this morning, we found the Peabody afloat and immediately after Breakfast, we received orders to prepare to imbark, which we did in the following manner: Companies A, D & part of Company C ware put in five squads, and the steam tug Pohick towed them. The rest of [the] Companies was put on board of a Schooner which was towed by another tug, whear we left the wharf at Hatteras at 9 ½ o'clock A.M. and arrived at the Peabody, which was about 3 miles from the shore, at 10 ¾ o'clock, and set sail for the field [at] 11 ¾ [o'clock], with the expectation of overtaking the fleet, which had left the inlet yesterday morning. Everything passed off smoothly until towards evening when a heavy fog arose & [it] also Commenced to rain, which prevented the steamer from running after night and, consequently, had to Cast anchor when within fifteen miles of New Bern, but ware in sight of the fleet. Lieut. Wood [B Co.] & myself had a state room, but Lieut. Bast [B Co.] took quarters in the fore Cabin. When anchored in the Neuse river, everything was quiet except for the signal of whistles which frequently blew for the safety of the boats, in regard to the heavy fog to prevent danger. I retired to bed early as we war near the line of the rebel fortifications & we war to attack in the morning.

Friday, March 14th, 1862
on board of the steamer George Peabody on [the] Neuse River, N.C.

On arising this morning, we found the fog still overspreading the river. Consequently, [we] did not start until rather late and, after having started and run for a while, we found ourselves hard aground at the instent [instant] the fog lifted, and we found ourselves and the vessel headed directly for the shore. After puffing and pulling for a while we got off and proceeded on our Course up the river and arrived whear the troops had landed during the night. The Captain of the Vessel received orders to run up to Johnston's Point and land the troops as soon as possible. By 11 ¾ o'clock, every man was ashore, when we formed line of battle. After which, we received orders to bring ammunition up to the battlefield as the battle had bin Commenced early in the morning and our infantry line was running short of ammunition. So, each Company Carried 8 boxes of ammunition, each Box Containing 1000 Rounds. Five Companies started & took the railroad whilst my Company was detailed to take the ammunition train up to the battle field by turnpike, which was indeed a very laborious task. We had to carry the ammunition out of the small boats ashore & got a team rigged up & I was to report to the ordinance officer for orders, and he was to provide me with a guide, and, on reporting, he said the ammunition was badly wanted & he had no guide to send with me. But, he gave me the directions and I sketched it off on my Diary & started with the ammunition. I had not gone more than ½ a mile until we had to Cross a Bridge & as the ammunition waggen [wagon] was on the bridge, it broke through and, as time was everything, as our army was engaged, I had the men to unload the ammunition at once & we got our waggon out & I repacked it and started off. I sent a messenger back to Johnston's Point, informing Lieut. [Daniel W.] Flagler [21st MA] of the occurence and that I was again on my way for the field, but before any more teams Could Cross this bridge, the pioneers would have to repair it.[19] Thear is no material hear. [You have to] bring it with you. We had to unload the team 4 times before we got to the Battlefield as the roads was in afull [awful] Condition with mud & [we] Carried the ammunition on our shoulders for 4 & 5 hundred yards. [The] Mud [was] nearly Knee deep. We arrived at the battle ground just as it was getting dusk and on entring [entering] the lines of the battle field I had to remove Quite a number of dead bodies in order to get through my train & [there were] Howitzers dismounted, and the men working the Howitzer died with the trail Rope in thear hands when they war advancing on the fortifications and, at which time, thear Howitzer was dismounted. The rebels lay pretty thick around, yet our troops was also pretty thick laing [laying] around but the scene of artillery horses and the distribution of artillery on the rebel side was an awful sight. Horses in particular, Could be seen in all Kinds of mangled forms and also men in the same way. I finally got to the entrance of the breastworks, when the 2 frunt leaders of the team got so deep in the mud that we had to help the horses out & [I] was compelled to leave a guard with the ammunition and leave it thear for the night. Captain [Lewis O.] Morris [1st US Arty.] did not get up until after 12 o'clock at night with his battry [battery], owing to his horses giving out. [20] Captain Colyer got through with 2 sections of his battry & passed me about 4 miles from the battle field.[21] We were too late for the battle, as the enemy had retreated at 1 o'clock and our army having the victory & won the battle. The rebel Breastworks was about one & a quarter mile in length & they had 16 pieces of field Artillery planted in posision [position] in the breastworks & they had on the left of thear a very fine fort named Thompson, having 13 seaboard mounted 32 lb. guns, some of which was rifled. 10 of theas guns bore on our navy & shipping in the river & 3 bore [on the] right flank & on [the] right oblique movement of our infantry at the Charging of the Breastworks but our troops made the Charge and suckseed [succeeded] in driving the enemy, they retreating, Leaving everything behind them. Thar [there] was 44 heavy guns & 18 pieces of field artillery Captured [along with] 150 prisoners and Several magazines with ordinance [ordnance] stores. We Camped in the open Battle field during the night without any shelter. I made a small [fire (?)].

Saturday, March 15th
Fort Ellis, New Bern, N.C.

Slept very little during the night on account of it raining and [it] also being rather Cool. This morning, after daylight, I made a visit over the battle field & thear was everything in the shape of accoutrements and arms, [and] men lying around in all Kinds of manner & forms and the rebels' acccoutrements [were] lying just as they left them & [where they] threw them to hasten thear retreat. One rebel I saw with his hand up to his mouth with the Cartridge between his teeth, in the act of biting it & he died. They lay for 4 miles this way, until they got on the Cars at New Bern. Among the 150 prisoners was a Colnal [Colonel Clark Moulton] Avery [33rd NC] was taken, who commanded the right wing of the fortifications, at which place he was taken prisoner and nearly all of the 150 prisoners was out of his reigmt. [regt.][22] The Col. was a fine looking fellow and a good looking soldier. His eye is enough to tell any one that he is a brave man. I asked Colonel Avery whear he was taken prisoner & he very gentlemanly told me & said "My friend, if my Comrades had proved [as] true to thear work as we did on the right, you would not have gotten the works so soon." The right of the works was the last to be taken. Our troops

BATTLE OF NEW BERNE, N.C.

SCALE

1/4 · 1/2 · 1 MILE

N
W — E
S

FT. LANE 3 GUNS

ATLANTIC 2ND N.O. GA. RAIL ROAD

TO NEW BERNE

OLD BEAUFORT ROAD

WEATHERBY ROAD

BLIND ROAD

CAVALRY   CAVALRY

BATTERY UNFINISHED

CASEMATE BATTERY 2 GUNS

4 GUN BATT. UNFINISHED

NEUSE RIVER

BRYCE CREEK

ROAD TO POLLOCKSVILLE

FELLED TIMBER

H 26TH 33CO 33CO

R E N O
9TH N.J. 51ST N.Y. 21ST MASS.

51ST PENN.

35TH 7TH 37TH 27TH

A B L FELLED TIMBER OBSTRUCTIONS

FT. THOMPSON 13 GUNS

P A R K E R
4TH R.I.
8TH CONN.
5TH R.I.
11TH CONN.

F O S T E R
10TH CONN. 23TH MASS.
23TH MASS. 27TH MASS.
HOWITZER 24TH MASS. 25TH MASS.
FT. DIXIE 4 24 P'D'RS

EVANS MILL POND

A Battery of Two 24 Pounders not finished in Time.
L Latham's Battery. **B** Brem's Battery. **H** Harding's Battery.

Drawn by Matt Pfister from
Battles and Leaders of the Civil War

had to surround this portion of the Line on 3 sides before he surrendered. I looked at him and his manly apearenc [appearance] & his gentlemanly behaviour brought the words of [Robert] Burns to my mind "a man is a man for augh that." I asked him if he had any Breakfast & he said no he had eaten nothing since yesterday morning. They were attacted [attacked] early in the morning and was engaged all day until he surrendered. I took my Haversack and gave him his Breakfast out of it and gave him a drink out of my Canteen. I asked him if he chewed & said he did but was entirely out. I gave him a plug of tobacco & he thanked me and took my name. They were all in a Brick Kiln, except the Colnal. We had no other place to put them at the time and they looked more like Indians then [than] white men with Brick dust. I bad [bade] the Colnel good by.

Sunday, March 16th, 1862
Fort Ellis, N.C.

Arose this morning and went out to view the fortifications, which appeared to be very formidable and almost impregnant [impregnable] as thear was a 64 lb. rifled gun [illegible] mounted in it, and they never fired a shot out of it, showing plainly that Cowardice was the Chief Cause of thear defeat. I gave the men liberty to go out foriging [foraging] and it was not long until we had 2 or 3 sheep & hogs in Camp & with the flour that we Captured & rye for Coffey [coffee] we managed to live very well during the day, and flap Jack was very prominent all over Camp. Weather very pleasant today. Retired early.

Monday, March 17th, 1862
Fort Ellis

This morning at 8 o'clock, we received orders to encamp in tents of the 51st P.V. [Pennsylvania Volunteers], near the bridge at the mouth of the River Trent, and was engaged the whole day in pitching tents & fixing up. I was detailed as officer of the day as soon as we arrived on the ground. Had Dress perad in the evening at 5 ½ o'clock. Orders ware read from the Brigade headquarters to the effect that no more than five men will be absent at any one time from camp.

Tuesday, March 18th
Camp Near New Bern

Sleep in our tents last night & got a pretty good night's rest. [LT] Bast [B Co.] attended roale [roll] Call this morning. After I was relieved, [1st] Lieut. [Charles] Kleckner [D Co.] and myself went over to the town of New Bern and thear we conversed with some bitter rebel ladies.[23] One, in perticular [particular], remarked that she Could blow Abe Linkon's [Lincoln's] Brains out with a pistol. We visited the town & then returned to Camp again. Weather pleasant.

Wensday, March 19th, 1862
Camp Near New Bern, N.C.

Rested very well last night. The weather was quite hazy and Cloudy this morning. I did not get into Camp in time for Company [drill] but was in Camp shortly afterwards. Lieut. Bast [B Co.] drilled the Company at Company perade. This afternoon, we received a mail from the north. Commenced to rain in the evening—very hard. I went to town immediately after supper.

Thursday, March 20th, 1862
Camp Near New Bern

Rained very hard nearly the whole night, yet I sleep very well. A shot was fired by the picket guard and the long roal [roll] was sounded by some of the Companies. I returned to camp this morning, being too late for the ferry boat last night. I had quite a lot of provisions for our mess. 4 men of the 11th Connecticut Regt. were out foraging last night when three of them was captured by the rebels and the fourth one made his escape. Cloudy all day and, every now & then, raining right smart.

Friday, March 21st, 1862
Camp Near New Bern

This morning at 10 o'clock, Lieut. Wood [B Co.] relieved [LT] Bast [B Co.]. I had no officers on drill with me as Bast was acting as adjitent [adjutant] on dress perade, our adjitent having gone to town & did not return in time. Nothing of note in Camp but Company drills & Regimental peraids.

Saturday, March 22nd, 1862
Camp Near New Bern

This morning Lieut. Col. [Lieutenant Colonel] Sigfried had Command of the regimental Drill—Bast [B Co.] acting as adjt. [adjutant].[24] I acted as officer of the day & Lieut. Wood [B Co.], being on guard & Bast, on police, we war all three on duty away from our Company at one time. Had no afternoon drill, giving the men an oppertunity [opportunity] to Clean up for tomorrow's inspection. Captain Pleasants [C Co.] took dinner with us. The 24th Mass. Regt. returned from Washington [NC], after having marched up through the streets of Washington playing "Yankee Doodle". They found the town evacuated.

Sunday, March 23rd, 1862
Camp Near New Bern

This morning broke forth very pleasant. At 9 o'clock, a Church Bell rang and that was the first bell to ring for Church to our hearing since we left Harrisburg some 6 months ago. Our pickets of Foster's Brigade was driven in, while 2 war Captured by mounted rebels. I, being officer of the day, Lieut. Bast [B Co.] Commanded at the inspection.

Monday, March 24th, 1862
Camp Near New Bern

Had our reguler [regular] morning drill, Commanded by Lieut. Col. Sigfried. Lieut. Bast [B Co.] went on board of the Commissary Vessel and purchased some provisions for our mess and took in some scotch ale—at 12 ½ Cents per glass. Col. Nagle received a leave of absence for twenty days and imbarked on the steamer New York which is to sail in a few days. Lieut. Col. Sigfried has Command of our regt. during the Col.'s Absence.

Tuesday, March 25th, 1862
Camp Near New Bern

This morning it was rather Cold for pleasure in Camp. [2nd] Lieut. [Randall H.] Rice [G Co.] of the 11th Connecticut Regt. paid us a visit, also Capt. Pleasants [C Co.], who remained & took dinner with us.[25] Captain [William W.] Potts' [D Co.] Colerd Servent was drownded by axcident [accident] by falling overboard from the ferry Boat.[26] 2 men from each Company was detailed to proceed to Beaufort, N.C. with one of [Gen. Ambrose] Burnside's aides.[27]

March 26th
Camp Near Trent Bridge

Arose early this morning & found the sky over Cast with Clouds & [it] Commenced to rain at 10 o'clock A.M. Lieut. Bast [B Co.] was detailed as officer of the guard. Our regimental Band, that we left behind at Hatteras, arrived hear today & took up quarters in Compny C tents until they will pitch thear own tents. 10 men from each Compny war detailed to go out foraging under Command of Captain [Daniel B.] Kauffman [A Co.].[28] They captured Sevrel [several] hundred bushels of Corn for [the] Goverment [government]. Our men brought 2 heffers [heifers] for our Compny.

March 27th, 1862
Camp Near Trent Bridge

This morning the sun arose in all its Brightness. We had a shower of hail yesterday afternoon. Lieut. Wood

[B Co.] relieved Bast [B Co.]. After guard mounting, I went over & Called on Gen. Burnside [about] procuring the Command of a Light field Battrey, but did not get a definite answer, but the matter was under the Gen I's Consideration. Bast [B Co.] had Comand of the Co. Koons & Isaac Lippman, the sutler, arrived today & erected thear stand at the river side.[29]

March 28th, 1862
Camp Near Trent Bridge

Weather very pleasant, Col. Sigfried gave the regt. a hard drill today on Double quick. Lieut. Wood [B Co.] was relieved of guard duty by [2nd] Lieut. [Alexander S.] Brown of Co. H.[30] Bast [B Co.] had Command of the police Squad. I was officer of the day. Gen. Burnside visited our Camp today in Compny with his Staff. Bast Commanded the Compny in the after noon. Thear was very little drilling [on account of] getting such a severe drill this morning. Captain Pleasants [C Co.] was with us to supper, after which he went on board of [the] Steamer Hussar, he having received a leave of absence for twenty days to go home. The Steamer is to sail tomorrow morning. We retired to bed rather late.

March 29th, 1862
Camp Near Trent Bridge

Lieut. Bast [B Co.], on the sick list, having a severe Coff [cough] & did not attend any of the Drills today and remained in his tent until evening. In the afternoon I received orders from Gen. Burnside to proceed to the Battle field & select a Light field Battrey from the Captured pieces [which we] Captured from the rebels in the Battle of New Bern on the 14th of March & then report to Genrel [General Jesse] Reno.[31] I went to the Battle field & thear found the Celebrated Rebel Captain Latham's field Battrey & selected one iron rifled 6 lb. gun, with the name of the maker stamped on [the] end of the trunnion, which was made by Noble & Sons, Georgia, who Carried on Business in Reading [PA] at one time; and one 6 lb. Brass rifled gun & 2 Brass 24 lb. Howitzers & 2 Brass 12 lb. Smooth Bore guns, all from the Latham Battry, except the 6 lb. iron gun. I reported the selection to Gen. Reno and he said the selection was very good & to prepare them ready for service as quick as possible & "thear would be an order issued by Genrel Burnside detaching you from your Regt. to Command this Battrey." Old Stones [unidentified] from Hatteras was with us this evening. Lieut. Wood [B Co.] & myself went over to New Bern on Business at 7 o'clock.

March 30th
Camp Near Trent Bridge

This morning we ware busy orginising [organizing] our Battrey. In the afternoon, Lieut. Bast [B Co.] & Myself proceeded to the Battle ground on a hand truck on the railroad with 4 privates in search of a Battrey waggon and Traviling [traveling] forge, but did not suckseed; however, we found the Caissons, which we will bring down tomorrow. We returned to Camp in the evening rather tired after our march.

March 31st
Camp Near Trent Bridge

This morning, Lieut. Bast [B Co.] went on as officer of the guard. We did not attend Genrel inspection this morning. [It was] held by Lieut. Col. Sigfried, he taking the same formation in inspection as a Bregider [brigadier] Genrel by reviewing his Battalion. In the afternoon, I took my Compny & proceeded to the battle ground with 5 hand railroad trucks & brought the Caissons, which we found yesterday & we found them in a fearful Condition. At one place, we found one gun sticking fast against a stump with the horses' throats Cut. We found another, in the breastworks in position, all stringed with blood & mixed with hair & pieces of flesh sticking to the gun & in most Cases the traces war all Cut & the horses taken with them in the retreat. The field pieces war run away from the Breast works regardless of [the] Roads & when they got [stuck] fast, [they] abandoned them in this way.

April 1st, 1862
Camp Near Trent Bridge, North Carlina [Carolina]

Arose early this morning & after Breakfast I had the first drill on our guns—the 6 field pieces & it reminded me of Fort Clark whear [where] we had acted as artillery for so long & our men felt quite Proud as each detachment whelled [wheeled] out of Compny line & took thear posision at thear respective guns. Thear was quite a number of our officers & soldiers of the 48th on the grounds, viewing the drill & it was quite a sucksess & at 9 o'clock A.M., I received an order from Gen. Reno ordering me to move with my Battrey at once & debark on Steamer & report to Gen. [John G.] Foster in the City of New Bern, North Carlina on detached service, and we at once prepared for the march.[32] I had Bast [B Co.] relieved from guard duty, who was relieved by [1st] Lieut. [George H.] Gressang [I Co.][33] Bast reporting to his Compny for duty, I placed him in Command of the men while Lieut. Wood [B Co.] & myself, with a portion of the men, taking some of the equipage to the Landing. The men returned to the Camp for the night. We visited Captain [James] Belger [Btty. F. 1st RI Lgt. Arty.] & his Battry & he was very pleasant & pleased to hear that we ware going to join them.[34] They are very Comfortably quartered. Retired to bed early.

April 2nd, 1862
New Bern, North Carlina

Got up early this morning & went to New Bern to make arrangements for transportation for my men & Battrey through the City of New Bern. I sent Lieut. Wood [B Co.] over to Capt. Morris's Battery [1st US Arty.] to procure a team and a Battery wagon and a Traviling Forge & had

Lieut. Bast [B Co.] in charge of the men & he had our tents struck & had them and the baggage taken down to the Landing. At 9 ½ o'clock, the Co. marched down to the Landing & on thear arrival, I had some of the Baggage put on Board of the steamer with a number of the guns & Landed at New Bern with part of my Co., the others remaining with Lieut. Bast at Trent Bridge Landing, as thear was Ceveral Regts. to be taken over & in Consequence, we did not get all our Battrey over until the afternoon, when we got all our Battrey together in the great city of New Bern. It is about as Large as Schuylkill Heaven in Schuylkill County. While our Battrey stood in the street of New Bern, it Created a great deal of excitement among the rebels of the town, having it printed in the Caissons:

"Captain Latham's Light Field Battery
of S. C. Army"

And, on board of the steamer our men had put on the following Card underneath:

"Captain Latham, S. C. Army
Superseded by Captain Wren
of 48th Regt. Pa. Vols. of U.S. Army"

This Card Created a great excitement & the enquery [inquiry] was "Who is the Captain Wren" & I was pointed out to parties Ceverel times. I did not feel as easy as I might have felt but among the throng, who did I meet but the rebel Colonal [Colonel] Avery, who was then a prisoner. [He] came up to me & shook hands & said he was exchanged & would have me go with him & take a drink. I thanked him & he saw that I was Cautious in my posision & he said, "Captain, Come. I will see that nothing will happen to you." & I looked him in the face & I saw the man meant [to be] friendly & [while] waiting to get the horses hitched up, I went & took a drink with him. It was about ½ a square away from my Battrey & he escorted me back to my Battrey all safe. I bid him good bye, [and said] that I was about to move. I moved up town & reported to Gen. Foster & he was very Pleasant & he ordered me to take a posision in [the] rear of the town & in line of Fort Totten, which is now being erected & take posision with my Battrey Covering the ground between the Trent & Neuse Rivers & arrange our guns so as to act with the gunboats on the Neuse & Trent Rivers. We then marched out to Fort Totten & I planted the two rifled guns—one on our right flank and one on our Left flank—as they ware 6 lb. guns & [had a] good range to act and Cause a Cross fire with the gunboats on the Neuse & Trent rivers. I planted the 2–24 lb. Howizters about 50 yards to the right & Left of the main road Leading to Goldsborough & planted the 2–126 lb. guns on our right & left in between the 24 lb. Howitzers and the 6 lb. rifled guns & in this posision we Could form a Cross fire with our line on Land & also with gun boats on the Neuse & Trent rivers. Having the pieces all in posision & a detachment for each piece, the balance of the Compny pitched thear tents in the rear of our line along the Goldsborough Road in rear of the town. The 103rd New York Regt. and [the] 2nd Maryland Regt. Came in today & Camped on the other side of the river. We had roale Call to night very early on account of the men being very tired.

April 3rd, 1862
Fort Totten, New Bern, N.C.

This morning we had all the guns manned & had our regular Drill on the guns. Thear being a charge in the 6 lb. rifled iron gun, I detailed Lieut. Bast [B Co.] & a detachment to take it to the river road & discharge it. Bast said it was a rebel Charge, having been loaded by the rebels the day of the Battle. This forenoon our Regt. was moved on this side of the river & Camped alongside & on the Left of us. I was out all day at the ordinance [ordance] department receiving ammunition to fill our Caissons full—as we had not a full Compliment. The Balance of our men that was left at Hatteras Inlet arrived today. We also received one new recruit today. Captain [H. A. M.] Filbert of Co. K arrived hear, he said, "to see the elephant."[35] Flannel being scarce in the ordinance ship, I received 20 flannel Blouses & we Cut them up & made Cartridge Bags for them.

April 4, 1862
Fort Totten, New Bern, N.C.

We arose early this morning & at 8 O'clock A.M. we had a drill. Gen. Foster & his aides brought Col. [James H.] Ledlie [3rd NY Arty.] to our Camp & instructed him to take two of our pieces and man them & that our Compny would be attached to thear regiment, the 3rd New York Artillery & [be] under Colonel Ledlie's Command.[36] I received 5 barrels of cannon powder from [the] ordinance department. Lieut. Bailey and Captain Southmayd [both A Co.] of the 11th Connecticut paid us a visit today. Gen. Burnside Rode past our Camp today on "Old Bob", who is well known in Camp.

April 5th, 1862
Fort Totten, New Bern, N.C.

We had but one drill today. The rest of the day was spent in Cleaning up for tomorrow's Inspection. Compny C of the 3rd Artillery of New York had a drill on 2 of our guns & acquitted themselves very poorly indeed as artillerists. Lieut. Bast [B Co.], who witnessed them drilling & told us of thear drilling said, "Why, Captain, our men can beat them all Hollow." We received our new uniforms from D. A. [David A.] Smith [former LTC of the 48th PA] from Pottsville.[37] They all fit very well. Col. Ledlie [3rd NY Arty.] was in our Camp this morning giving some orders Concerning ammunition for our pieces. Lieut Bast & myself visited Fort Totten & the fortifications & which appears to be very formidable & when finished will be a very fine fort. It is being built with the Labour of the Counter bands [contrabands], who has a mark of distinction—a piece of white muslin on thear hats & on it is in Black Large letters "U.S.". Any one Coming in Contact with that will have to get out of the way.

It is quite a treat to be on the ground at roale Call of theas darks. They have roale Call at eavry [every] meal & thear is a darkey Captain to each Squad & he superintends the roale Calling. Thear is some siantifick [scientific] names which our men have copied as follows:

> George Washington Harris
> Henry Clay Thompson
> Thomas Harrison Johns
> Williams Webster Thomas
> Henry Windfield Scott Samson
> Henry Harrison Jackson

& thear answer admitted them to get thear rashons.

April 6th, 1862
Fort Totten, New Bern, N.C.

The weather was very pleasant & warm. Had inspection & ameditly [immediately] after inspection we received mail. We occupied the day in answering Letters. The 24th Regt. of Mass. Vols. gave a kind of a Matinee in frunt of Gen. Burnside's quarters.

April 7th, 1862
Fort Totten, New Bern, N.C.

We arose early this morning & at 8 o'clock had a Drill on the field pieces, after which, I went & Called on Col. Ledlie [3rd NY Arty.] that my Compny would be transferred from the 48th Penn. vols. to the 3rd New York Artillery Vol. I received a reguler routine of duty & also Copies of artillery tack-tick [tactics]. The Col. made me a personal present of a Copy of field artillery tackticks in 2 Volumes which can be Carried in your pocket. Had a Drill at 2 o'clock on the guns. Despenced [dispensed] with dress peraid according to the routine duty & had roale Call instead.

April 8th, 1862
Fort Totten, New Bern, N.C.

The weather being very pleasant this morning, we had our reguler drill on the field pieces. Lieut. Bast [B Co.] visited the 48th & witnessed the regt. under the Command of Lieut. Col. Sigfried & pronounced the movements very good in his estimation & after dinner, he started out to visit the 11th Connecticut. On his way, he met Capt. Southergood [probably Capt. Southmayd of the 11th CT], who told him that they had bin paid & on his [Bast's] return home, he Came a different route & Came in the direction he had ranged the 6 lb. rifled gun to fire the shot out of & he found the tracks of it [the shot] through the Limbs about ½ a mile from whear he had the gun planted. I visited Col. Ledlie [3rd NY Arty.] this afternoon and had quite a pleasant time with him.

April 9th, 1862
Fort Totten, New Bern, N.C.

Last night it Commenced to rain & Continued all night & today [it was] pouring down in perfit [perfect] torrents at times. Consequently, we had no Drill. In the afternoon, we received out pay Roales & had the men sign them— ready for tomorrow for the paymaster when he makes his appearance to hand over the green backs, which is much needed.

April 10th, 1862
Fort Totten, New Bern, N.C.

It cleared up last night. We had a drill this morning and amediatley after which the paymaster Came & payed and [we] had no Drill in the afternoon, [thereby] giving the men a little time to settle up thear little accounts. Some of the men got passes to go to town & got drunk & on thear returning to Camp got put in the guard house.

April 11, 1862
Fort Totten, New Bern, N.C.

Last night, at about 11 o'clock, we ware awakened with a Drunken Squall held in the sergeants' tent. I went out & to my surprise & disgust I found Captain Kauffman of Co. A of the 48th & Lieut. Gressang [I Co.] in the muss. After they ware dispersed, Corporal [Joseph] Johnston [B co.] became very noisy.[38] So I had him taken to the 3rd Artillery guard house. I received orders today to report to the 48th Regt. again & Lieut. Col. Sigfried & myself Called on Gen. Reno in regard to our Battry & we ware assured that the Battry would be attached to Reno's Brigade. Lieut. Bast [B Co.] expressed the men's money home today to thear respective families.

April 12th, 1862
Fort Totten, New Bern, N.C.

Weather very pleasant. Lieut. Bast [B Co.] went on as officer of the guard. Toward evening, he had trouble with a lot of Drunken men of Compny C. Having Bin Fighting, they ware put in the guard House & they had to be tied hand & foot. They are Bombarding Fort Macon today. Today is the day that the first blow was struck one year ago of this war.

April 13th, 1862
Fort Totten, New Bern, N.C.

Weather very pleasant until evening, when it Commenced to rain. After being relieved as officer of the day, I had the horses hitched up to the small piece & went into the field to practise [practice] field movements & in the afternoon, [we] had 2 pieces out—one of them by hand—& had a reguler field Drill, [with] the men doing very well. In the afternoon, we received a stack of new arms—being Enfield Rifles—but we did not Distribute them, owing to the lateness of the day.

April 14th, 1862
Fort Totten, New Bern, N.C.

This morning we arose early and distributed the muskets & accoutrements to the men & at 7 ½ o'clock, we received orders to have one day's rashons Cooked, with arms & accoutrements in good condition, as we ware likely to Leave this afternoon. Consequently, the morning Drill on the guns was dispenced with. Amediately after dinner orders Came Countermanding the anticipated March & we had our regular Compny Drill in the afternoon. We had Dress peraid in the evening & we Boxed up during the day the old accoutrements & turned them over to [the] Quartermaster.[39] Gen. Foster paid us a visit & Lieut. Wood [B Co.] accompanied him to town.

April 17th, 1862
Fort Totten, New Bern, N.C.

The weather [was] very warm all day. Lieut. Col. Sigfried took the regt. out on Drill & he took them through right Smart. The Majority of the officers ware Complaining Considerable about the Drill being too hard. However, we [B Co.] ware not in it as we Drilled on the Cannon. I received Shoes & Blouses for the men. I had them distributed in the afternoon. In the evening, the men was very merry, George Marsden [B Co.] and [Thomas] Conell [B Co.] ware playing the violin while the others war dancing in the Company street.[40] Had our reguler dress peraid.

April 18th, 1862
Fort Totten, New Bern, N.C.

We arose early this morning. I went on as officer of the day at 9 o'clock by request of Lieut. Col. Sigfried. We accompanied the Regt. on Regimental Drill. It was for us to say whether we would go or not. Being detached from the Regt. & in the artillery service, but having a pride in our regt., we Complied with the request & went & the regimental drill was the practising [of] firing by the Snapping of Caps & [we] went through Severel field movements, which they done very well. This evening, I called a meeting of the member's of the old Washington Artillery of Pottsville, of which I was Captain & we Celebrated our first anniversery [anniversary] of our march through Baltimore for the protection of the National Capital, [which was] in response to the President's Call for volunteers. Col. Nagle arrived hear this evening, returning from his 20 days Leave of Absence & Joined his Regt.

April 19th, 1862
Fort Totten, New Bern, N.C.

The weather was very pleasant all day. Lieut. Bast [B Co.] went on as officer of the guard at 8 o'clock, relieving [2nd] Lieut. [Henry] Boyer [H Co.].[41] Col. Nagle occupied the forenoon in looking around Camp & expressed himself & was gratified in seeing everything in such good order. About 20 Counterband arrived hear from little Washington, N.C. & gave information to the effect that the Rebels was fortifying themselves very strong in the vicinity of Washington and that they ware going to make a desperate stand. The Rebels, according to the darkeys' accounts, has severel Regt. of pressed troops thear which they intend to force to fight. Col. Nagle had Command of Dress peraid this evening.

April 20th

Nothing of note today, Sunday, except inspection by Col. Nagle & Dress peraid in the evening.

April 21st, 1862
Fort Totten, New Bern, N.C.

A heavy wind was prevailing all day which filled the air full of Dust. At 11 o'clock the New fortifications was dedicated by [the] raising of the flag & [by] firing a National salute and [by] a review by Gen. Foster of the 3rd Artillery of New York, which turned out to be anything but a magnificent Sight. In the first place, they made a [mistake] in firing the salute by one squad Not ramming home their Cartridge & then damaging the piece & declaring that it was half spiked & in the second place, in marching in review & forming line, they made another Botch & it was plainly to be seen that the Gen. was entirely out of Patience with [them].

April 22nd
Fort Totten, New Bern, N.C.

Very Cold all day. Lieut. Wood [B Co.] went on as officer of the guard. We had regimental drill, Col. Nagle Commanding. After dinner, [the] Col. got out the police and [they] was under his personal superintendence & gave the Camp a thorough policing. About the middle of the afternoon, the 51st Pa. Vols. returned to thear Camp from the Dismal Swamp, whear they had a small engagement with the enemy, whereby they lost 17 men which they had to leave on the ground as they were obliged to retreat in great haste or suffer to be Captured by the rebels who war strongly reinforced during the conflict. The enemy had a Battry of 6 rifled pieces. The New York 9th Regt. was also in the engagement & showed both Bravery & Cowardice. Had Dress peraid in the evening

April 23rd
Fort Totten, New Bern, N.C.

Weather very pleasant. I went on as officer of the day at 9 o'clock A.M. The Col. had a regimental Drill. Lieut. Bast [was] in Command of my Compny. The Col. drilled the men very hard but they all appeared to like it. We had our reguler Drill in the afternoon on [the] field pieces. Colnal Nagle was, today, appointed and made a Brigadier Genrel & the Regt. will be under [the] Command of Lieut. Col. Sigîried. Genrel Nagle appointed adigent [Adjutant John] Bertolette of the 48th Regt. Pa. Vols. as a Genrel of his Staff

& Lieut. Col. Sigfried has made the following selection for his Command. Lieut. O. C. Bosbyshell of Co. G was relieved from acting Quartermaster [and] was made adigent & Lieut. Bast of Compny B was made Quartermaster & [they] will enter upon thear respective duties tomorrow. Gen. Nagle Commands the first Brigaid of [the] second Division, [which is] commanded by Gen. Reno. Col. [Edward] Ferrero was also made [an acting] Brigadier Genrel & has Command of the 2nd Brigade of [the] 2nd division, [which is] under Command of Gen. Reno.[42] The first Brigade Consists [of the] 48th Regt. Pa. Vols., [the] 103rd New York, [the] 9th New Jersey & [the] 2nd Meryland [Maryland].

April 24th, 1862
Fort Totten, New Bern, N.C.

Lieut. Bast, [B Co.] having bin appointed Quartermaster, Commenced in his duty as such this morning. A Rebel Colonal Came into our lines this morning & gave himself up to Gen. Burnside. Gen. Nagle made his headquarters in the 48th [PA] for the present. We received a magazine for ammunition.

April 25, 1862
Fort Totten, New Bern, N.C.

Received from our New Quartermaster some very Nice Light Blue Britches for the men & had them distributed & the men had them on at dress peraid & [they] looked well. Lieut. Col. Sigfried had the Regt. out on Drill and gave them one of his old fashioned Drills of Double Quick & Oblique squads, which the men are down on like a thousand of Bricks. This afternoon a Schooner of Subsistence arrived bringing Isaac Lippman, Lieut. James of Co. F., Corporal [Edward H.] Sillyman [G Co.] & [Nelson] "Snaper" Drake [K Co.] from Hatteras Inlet.[43] Surgeon Reber of the 48th Regt. was appointed Brigade Surgeon of the first Brigaid, 2nd Division under Gen. Nagle.

April 26th, 1862
Fort Totten, New Bern, N.C.

Waked up this morning by a heavy sound of rain and had [rain] during the day. Lieut. James [F Co.] stayed with us tonight. This forenoon, Gen. Nagle moved his quarters to town. We received some express from home, which was brought into Camp & Paul Sheck [B Co.], receiving a Case Containing Liquor & [it] was drunk by the German friends & by 9 o'clock this evening, they got a quarreling & a number had to be put in the guard house.[44] We received the news of Fort Macon having bin taken by Burnside's troops under [the] Command of Gen. [John G.] Parke & my old friend, Capt. Morris [1st US Arty.] acted as Chief of artillery during the Bombardment & Lieut. George Gowen of Co. C Commanded a gun during the bombardment & Dismounted a rebel gun in the fort with his piece [for] which he received quite a Compliment from Gen. Parke.[45] The troops stationed outside, in the Direction of Goldsborough, have all Called in, merely leaving the pickets out. Ceveral Rebel Deserters came in our lines yesterday.

27th April, 1862
Fort Totten, New Bern, N.C.

Weather still Cloudy. At 8 o'clock [we] had inspection, Lieut. Bast [QM] appearing with the staff for the first time. After inspection Lieut. Bast & Myself took a walk into the Country for Ceverel miles and, on our return, we found Mr. Miller of Louisiana in our quarters and we had hin to take dinner with us. The 3rd New York Artillery fired a national salute in Honer [honor] of the Capture of Fort Macon on Friday. The firing was poor as they fired too eregular [irregular]. Gen. Nagle viewed our dress peraid & appeared to be well pleased with it.

April 28th, 1862
Fort Totten, New Bern, N.C.

The weather very Cool this morning. Gen. Burnside and the Prisners [prisoners] that was taken at Fort Macon arrived hear this afternoon. Thear is Considrable [considerable] dissatisfaction existing among the troops against Burnside for relieving all those rebel Prisoners on peroale [parole].

April 29th, 1862
Fort Totten, New Berne, N.C.

Thear was nothing of note today except Drilling.

April 30th

We had no drill for the purpose of Cleaning up for muster; review & inspection by Gen. Nagle & Staff. After the review & inspection, the Gen. paid us a very high Compliment & said he had seen nothing in new Bern to Compare with it. Lieut. Bast [QM] spent the evening with Capt. Pleasants [C Co.] & had a very pleasant time.

May 1st, 1862
Fort Totten, New Bern, N.C.

Owing to it raining all day, all Drills was suspended. We received 10 days rashons in our Compny today. This does not look like moving. Lieut. Bast [QM] received an order from Lieut. Col. Sigfried for 2 horses—one for himself as Quartermaster & one for Bosbyshell as adigentent [adjutant].

May 2nd, 1862
Fort Totten, New Bern, N.C.

This morning Broak [broke] forth with a Clear sky & had the appearance of a May day. I received a large mail today, which Came with the steamer George Peabody.

Compny H was out firing [at] Target today & brought good target. My Compny goes out tomorrow. Quartermaster [William] Auman [G Co.] went out scouting with a Company of the 103rd New York & Quartermaster Sergeant [Jacob] Wagner went out with the team & brought in some forage.[46] Two of our pickets was shot this afternoon by the rebels— one of them killed instantly, the other Very Badly wounded. Gen. Nagle & his staff viewed our Dress peraid.

May 3rd, 1862
Fort Totten, New Bern, N.C.

The weather was very warm all day. I took the Compny out to practise with the muskets on the target but they did not make a very good target. [The] distance fired was 150 yards & 200 yards. After dress peraid, Capt. Pleasants [C Co.] & Lieut. Bast [QM] took a horse back ride with out horses of the Battrey.

May 4th, 1862
Fort Totten, New Bern, N.C.

The weather was still warm until 3 o'clock, when it rained & Cooled the earth & atmostpier [atmosphere]. This morning I went on duty as officer of the day. We had Regimental inspection. Lieut. Col. Sigfried intends to peraid the regt. through town tomorrow. Received News of New Orleans being taken by our forces.

May 5th, 1862
Fort Totten, New Bern, N.C.

Arose this morning & [it] was raining very hard & Continued all day. [We] had no Drilling or dress peraid. The Quartermaster, Bast, received the Clothing for the Compnys at Hatteras & brought them up to this Camp to be ready for them when they join the regt. again.

May 6th, 1862
Fort Totten, New Bern, N.C.

We ware awakened this morning by a fearful thunder storm & the rain pouered [poured] down in torrents. The guard that was out on duty took off thear Bayonets as the Lightning fairly hissed over them. The Lightning struck into a tree in town whear a sentinel was standing & it sent him a Kicking. The darkies have a Kind of superstition that thear was a heavy battle Fought yesterday which Caused the trouble of the elements. I had command of the Regimental drill this morning for the first time & I was very Cautious in taking such moves as I understood thoroughly & we got along very well & the Compnys ware all well pleased. We drilled reguler & not 2 long. [With] Lieut. Wood [B Co.] being on guard, & Lieut. Bast. [the] acting Quartermaster & Myself, [the] acting Colnal, Lieut. Brown of Compny H Commanded my Compny. The Lieut. Col. took the regt. down through the town on a street peraid & they made a very fine appearance.

May 7th, 1862
Fort Totten, New Bern, N.C.

The weather was very pleasant. Thear was a detail from the diffrent [different] Compnys to dig a well which was ordered by the Sanitary Commission, under Lieut. Bast [QM]. After dinner, the Captains of the diffrent Compnys of the regt. made a request to have sack coats issued to the noncommissioned officers of our regt. The steamer John Farnnan arrived from the North, Bringing with her a very large mail, [and] also the recruiting party which has bin gone 2 months. Sergeant [Thomas] Johnson of our Compny, who was one of the party, appeared to be very glad to Join his Compny.[47] He is still the same old Tom & by this mail we received the good & glorious news of the evacuation of Yorktown & [General George B.] McClellan [is] in hot pursuit after the enemy. [QM] Sergeant [Charles W.] Schnerr and our Chaplen [Chaplain Samuel A. Holman] arrived hear from Hatteras Inlet on a visit.[48]

May 8th, 1862
Fort Totten, New Bern, N.C.

The weather still remains very pleasant. Lieut. Col. Sigfried had Regimental drill. [I had] the New Clothing for the troops of the 48th [PA] on Hatteras put on board of [a] vessel today to go to them. The sanatary [sanitary] well is down some 14 feet in depth. Old Paul Sheck [B Co.] & 3 of the Germans war in town today and got too much Liquor & they had a Quarrel among themselves.

May 9th, 1862
Fort Totten, New Bern, N.C.

The weather still very pleasant. This morning our regiment [regiment] was formed at 7 o'clock & was ordered to march to the other side of the river for a Brigaid Drill. [It] Came off tolarable [tolerable] well for a new Brigaid. Quartermaster Bast visited the artillery Barracks to get two horses for the regt. but he got only one, the stock being very low. Thear is to be 10 days rasions [rations] to be issued tomorrow. We went to bed very early tonight, being tired.

May 10th, 1862
Fort Totten, New Bern, N.C.

Thear was nothing of note in Camp today. Drilling & Cleaning up for inspection tomorrow. The Companies received 10 days rashons. Commissary Sergeant Schnerr left for Hatteras today on board of [a] vessel.

May 11th, 1862
Fort Totten, New Bern, N.C.

By order of Lieut. Col. Sigfried, the inspection [was] at 7 o'clock A.M. The weather was very pleasant during the day. Ceverel Companies of Cavalry & a Company of Light artillery arrived hear. [They] Landed & Marched across the river to encamp at the Barracks of the rebel Cavalry, which were captured.

May 12th, 1862
Fort Totten, New Bern, N.C.

I received some Clothing for my Compny & had it issued to the men. I had two of our men discharged. [John] Williams & [David W.] Molsen, being Mulattoes & sent them north by Steamer.[49]

May 13th, 1862
Fort Totten, New Bern, N.C.

Today Ceverel Artillery Companies belonging to this department had target practise & thear was a Constant roar & Bombing of Cannon. The Compny in fort totten done some very good firing. After dinner a Captain of artillery, who came in yesterday at the request of Captain [Joseph H.] Hoskings [F Co.] at Fort Hatteras, Came to see us.[50] The Boat, Alice Price, Came in from the north bringing special Dispatches to Gen. Burnside. We war promised new Sibley tents tomorrow from the Quartermaster.

May 14th, 1862
Fort Totten, New Bern, N.C.

This morning a review took place, at 8 o'clock, of the Cavalry & artillery. They ware reviewed across the river at the old Secesh Barracks. Lieut. Bast [QM] went to town to try to get the horse I had but did not suckseed in procuring him. I was very sorry as he was a perfect feet [fit] with myself & the men & I was sorry to part with him. I have received orders to turn in my Battry & all equippage into the 3rd New York Artillery by order of Col. Ledlie, Chief of Artillery.

May 15th, 1862
Fort Totten, New Bern, N.C.

Today the 2nd Meryland & Ceverel Companies of Cavalry went out in the direction of Goldsborough to Capture some rebel Cavalry which are prowling around & engaging our pickets & this evening they went and a skirmish followed & Ceverel rebels [were] killed & one [was] made a prisoner. I turned in my Battry today to Col. Ledlie of the 3rd N.Y. Artillery. Lieut. Wood [B Co.] went on as officer of the guard. The Regt. had no Drill today nor dress peraid owing to the weather being very rainy.

May 16th, 1862
Fort Totten, New Bern, N.C.

We received our Sibley tents today—5 tents to each Compny. We had a regmental [regimental] drill this afternoon, by Lieut. Col. Sigfried, of 2 hours duration. According to the routine of duty by Gen. Nagle, the Regt. has 5 hours' Drilling each day, which Causes a Considerable amount of dissatisfaction among the men as they think that they are perfect in Drilling.

May 17th, 1862
Fort Totten, New Bern, N.C.

Last night Ceverel Companies of Cavalry & Artillery, about one o'clock, marched out on the Neuse Road. We also heard the long roale beaten at that time. During the day, we heard of a skirmish which took place this morning by which Ceverel of our men was wounded.

May 18th, 1862
Fort Totten, New Bern, N.C.

Sunday. [We] had Regimental inspection this morning at 7 o'clock. We received bread for our men this morning, which I Called the doctor's attention to it & he had it Condemned, being sour. After inspection, Captain Pleasants [C Co.] & Lieut. Bast [QM] & myself took a ride on horseback. We went to the 10th Connecticut & became acquainted with a [few] of the Captains. One Captain [Joseph W.] Branch [F Co.] accompanied us from thear Camp.[51] We war overtook with a Compny of Cavalry, who, with a flag of truce, war going out with prisoners to have an exchange which ware prisoners of war [and] also to escort some ladies across the lines of our Sentinels. Bast did not enjoy his ride, as the horse he had wanted to be always ahead & [it] was very hard to hold & [it] rushed into Brush with him Ceverel times. We returned to Camp at 3 o'clock P.M.

May 19th, 1862
Fort Totten, New Bern, N.C.

We had no Drill owing to pitching our new Sibley tents & we shifted the whole Camp Back to the rear in order to give more peraid ground in frunt. A steamer arrived from the North Bringing a very large mail. Captain Morris [1st US Arty.], having returned from Fort Macon, Called upon me to ascertain what was done with my Battrey & I told him I had turned it into Col. Ledlie, 3rd New York Artillery by order of Gen. Burnside.

May 20th, 1862
Fort Totten, New Bern, N.C.

Lieut. Bast [QM] [is] still under the weather from his ride to the picket Line on Sunday. We received rashions for the Compny. The Col. dispensed with all drilling today, Giving the men a Chance to fix up thear tents & arrange thear quarters. We had dress peraid at the usual time.

May 21st, 1862
Fort Totten, New Bern, N.C.

[A] Complaint being made to the Col. that 5 tents to a Compny was not sufficient for the Number of men, the

Lieut. Colnal had a requisition filled for ten more Sibley tents and [had it] approved by Gen. Reno & Gen. Nagle. This Morning, Quartermaster Auman [G Co.] took three Companies of the 103rd New York Regt. & proceded to Hatteras Inlet to relieve the 4 Compnys of the 48th Regt. Pa. Vols. Major Sherman [unit?] Came hear and paid off our Reigment [regiment] up to April 30th, 1862.

May 22nd, 1862
Fort Totten, New Bern, N.C.

The weather was very pleasant. We received the additional Sibley tent & had it pitched. We war busy making up packages of money to send home by express to the men's families and friends.

May 23rd, 1862
Fort Totten, New Bern, N.C.

At seven o'clock this morning, under Command of the Lieut. Col., our regt. marched across the river to perticipate [participate] in a Brigade Drill under Gen. Nagle. While we were over, we war Caught in a heavy showr [shower] of rain & thoroughly drenched down. At one o'clock, the 4 Compnys of the 48th arrived from Hatteras Inlet & drived in Camp & Joined the reigment so we now have our regment [regiment] together again, which makes all hands feal [feel] good.[52]

May 24th, 1862
Fort Totten, New Bern, N.C.

This morning we received an issue of Fresh meat, which is quite a treat to the men. This evening the whole Regment appeared on dress peraid & made a very nice Line. The 10 Compnys had not bin together for ten weaks [weeks].

May 25th, 1862
Fort Totten, New Bern, N.C.

Being short of wood & raining nearly all day, the Quartermaster was hunted up sharp by the Cooks. Towards evening, the rain abated & the Lieut. Col. had dress peraid.

May 26th, 1862
Fort Totten, New Bern, N.C.

This morning at seven o'clock we had a regimental drill, when Lieut. Bosbyshell of Co. G, who was acting as Adigent [adjutant] Came very near meeting with a serious accident. The horse he rode became bucky & Commenced to rair [rear] on his hind feet & threw himself on his back [with] Bosbyshell Coming underneath. Being rainy, we had no Dress peraid.

May 27th, 1862
Fort Totten, New Bern, N.C.

Sleep very little all night as the rain poured down in perfict [perfect] torrents & with a very strong wind, which Blew down the fly which we had in frunt of our Marquee. It was one of the hardest rain storms we have experienced since we Came to New Bern. Lieut. Kleckner of Co. D was reprimanded by Gen. Nagle for interfering with the mule team & the Quartermaster the other day. We had no regimental Drill today on account of [the] rain. Lieut. Bosbyshell was promoted from the rank of 2nd Lieut. to the rank of 1st Lieut. and [it] was read at Dress peraid [that he was] to be obeyed accordingly. [Acting] Lieut. Curtis Pollock, having a commission from [PA] Governor [Andrew] Curtin in his possession, of 2nd Lieut., was not recognized by the staff officers & was not read off to the rigment [regiment], as it ought to have bin done with Bosbyshell's filling the vacancy.[53]

May 28th, 1862
Fort Totten, New Bern, N.C.

The weather was very warm. Isaac Lippman is going to open a store in New Bern. Today, a salute of 16 guns was fired from Fort Totten in honor of the arrival of the Honorable Edwin Stanton, the appointed governor of this state. Received orders to move across the river with our regt. tomorrow.

May 29th, 1862
Camp near River Trent, N.C.

We arose early this morning & after Breakfast [we] Commenced packing up to move & soon the teams arrived. One was assigned to each Compny. Each team brought three loads and the Camp is only about ½ moved. Some of the Captains made Complaints about the Quartermaster not using the Compaynes [companies] all alike, which was impossible. He could only give them what he received. The New Camp is situated on [the] North side of the railroad & on the south side of the Trent River. It is a very nice Camping ground. 6 of the teams, when near the Camping ground, stuck fast & had to be unloaded, the soil being sandy & swampy.

May 30th, 1862
Camp Near River Trent, N.C.

This morning was busy [with us] trimming & fixing up our New Camp & [with the] the Quartermaster Landing the stores of the Commissary in boats as the roads yesterday, to our Camp, was Cut up so much that they Could not be used today.

May 31st, 1862
Camp Near River Trent, N.C.

The Regt. formed Line this morning for the purpose of attending the review of the 2nd division, Commanded by

Gen. Reno, but was postponed, on account of the rain, until 4 o'clock P.M.. The reviewing officers were Gen. Burnside's & Governor Stanton, as Commander in Chief of state, accompanied [them]. Then the review was a splendid affair & the 48th Regt. of Pa. Vols. took the praise in Line of Brigade, which made our boys feel like Roosters. Fred [Frederick J.] Brown & William Maize, members of the Band, received thear Discharges & left [for the] Rear on [a] steamer Bound North.[54]

June 1st, 1862
Camp Near River Trent, N.C.

After Breakfast we had monthly inspection, after which [the] Compnys received thear issue of Rasions from the Quartermaster. We received a mail from the north, which was always a welcome visitor. Today, I had a private Visit from Lieut. Curtis Pollock of Compny G & when he Came into my Marquee, he sat down and was so full that he burst into tears and I said, "Lieut., what is wrong?" "Well, I have come in for your advice in relation to my case as a Lieutenant. Do you think I can hold it?" I replied, "Yes, you are the 2nd Lieutenant of Compny G of the Regt. of Pa. Vols. and you have your Commission from governor Curtin, the Commander in Chief of Penna., & [it] Cannot be Laid aside by Regimental officers. Gen. Nagle & myself has had a pretty warm interview in relation to your Case & he wished to Know from me why I favored you in taking the posision of 2nd Lieut. I told him by your Commission from Governor Curtin of Penna. 'Yes, but he was not entitled to it according to reguler Promotion.' 'Why, Gen.,' said I, 'thear is no reguler promotion in the 48th Regt. or your Brother, Daniel Nagle, of Co. D, Would Not fill your position of Major of this Reigment over the heads of [the] Captains of Compny A, B & C of this regment. Gen., I hope you will excuse me, but Right is Right & Rong [wrong] is Rong & as a military officer I must say, as thear is no reguler line of Promotion in the 48th Regt., Lieut. Pollock Cannot be laid aside." I told Pollock if I was in his place, I would equip myself in the rank of 2nd Lieut. & take my Posision in the Compny & he said he had no money to equip. I told him I Could lend him a sword & a Coat & I loaned him money to go & buy a pair of 2nd Lieut.'s shoulder straps & he rigged himself up & appeared in uniform & it was quite a talk in Camp & some remarked, "He will be ordered out of Line." "Well," said I, "I would not like to be the officer to issue the order." So Curt appeared & was recognized as [the] 2nd Lieut. of Compny G & he was a firm friend of mine afterward. The Col. of the Regt. then had an order read that all promotions would be in reguler form of promotion in the Line [of the] Regt. hearafter.

June 2nd, 1862
Camp Near River Trent, N.C.

Thear was nothing of note in Camp today, except Drilling & the Chatring [chattering] of Lieut. Pollock's [G Co.] appearance. I told Pollock, "It is your duty to study the tacticks & get Booked up or you might be reducd to the Ranks again."

June 3rd, 1862
Camp Near River Trent, N.C.

Today the review of the 1st Division, under Command of Gen. Foster, was to Come off at 10 o'clock A.M., but was postponed until the afternoon at 4 o'clock & it was not as grand [an] affair as was expected as this division is reported to Consist of all Crack Regts. from the east. The division, Combined, Consisted of 6 Reigments of infantry, 8 pieces of Boat howitzers, manned by Marines, & [a] regt. of artillery & one Reigment of Cavalry. Thear marching was very good. This evening, Lieut. Gowen of Compny C, who has bin detached from the regment for some time, has again rejoined his Compny. 2 hundred men & one Captain & 4 Lieutenants was detailed to do Provost duty over in New Bern. Lieut. Wood [B Co.], being one of the Lieuts., Leaves me all alone in the officer line.

June 4th, 1862
Camp Near River Trent, N.C.

Last night at 9 o'clock it Commenced to rain & it rained the whole night. Last night the 24th Mass. Regt. embarked on Board of [a] steamer to proceed to Little Washington [because of] news reaching hear that our picket war enoyed [annoyed] Considerable by the enemy. The provost guard was relieved this morning by the 25th Mass. Regt. & the old guard received quite a Compliment from the Citizens of the town for keeping such good order during the review.

June 5th, 1862
Camp Near Trent River, N.C.

We passed a rather restless night, being enoyed with Mosquitoes. We had fresh Beef issued to the men today. A detail was made from our Regt. today of ten privates & two noncommissioned [officers] to guard Gen. Reno's Quarters. Fred Knittle of my Compny was one of the privates.[55] Lieut. Col. Sigfried had a regimental Drill & [he] wound [it] up in a Dress peraid.

June 6th, 1862
Camp Near River Trent, N.C.

Brigade Drill was ordered for today, but owing to it raining in the morning, it was dispensed with until the afternoon & [we] had Dress peraid in the evening.

June 7th, 1862
Camp Near River Trent, N.C.

Weather still Cloudy & Nasty. Major Nagle had the Regt. today on Regmental Drill & made a poor show of it. He got the Companies all mixed up & he found he could not get them out & [he] Consulted Capt. Kauffman [A Co.] & he acted according to Kauffman's instructions & he found it made things no better & he then Consulted Captain [Jo-

seph A.] Gilmour [H Co.] & he said he Could take them out
& the Major gave Gilmour's Command & [he] Still was
mixed up & Captain [John R.] Porter [I Co.] spoke up &
Said he believed Captain Wren Could bring us out, if it was
possible to be done. So the Major rode down to the Left of
the Regt. on his Hatteras horse & Said, "Captain, we're in
a little mix up."[56] "Yes," said I, "we are." "Well," said he,
"what Command wood [would] you give to get out?" "Well,
Major, I have a Command that will bring you all right, but
you will not find it in the tacticts [tactics]. "Well," said he,
very short & Crusty, "what is it?" "I would give the Command 'by the Companies—untangle,'" & he wheeled his
horse & went back to the group of Officers & was asked what
Wren said. "Why, he says he'd give the Command 'by Companies—untangle.'" and they snigred [snickered] & laughed
among themselves & he finely [finally] adopted the same
thing, ordering Compny A to take a posision & ordered the
Companies to take thear proper posision on Company A &
it was then you Could see the movement of untangle made
by one Compny going to the right & some to the left to get
into thear proper places. I was mortified to see our reigment
in this Muddle as Gen. Foster & staff was viewing the drill
of a number of Reigments that was out drilling. The Major
then marched us home & on our way home I met Col. Sigfried. "Well," said he, "how did you get along today?" & I
told him, "slecht" [Pennsylvania German for "Bad" or "no
good"] and he Bursted out Laughing & he said he had seen
us & "Whear was you?" said I. "I was setting on my horse
on the road near the Left of your line." "Why, then did you
not Come & help a fellow out?" He said he was attending a
Genrel Court Martial. "Well," said I, "don't mention our
Case thear."

June 8th, 1862
Camp Near River Trent, N.C.

Sunday, Lieut. Col. Sigfried held the reguler inspection during the day. 7 Bodies ware brought in hear for
burial, belonging to the 24th Mass. Regt., from Washington,

N.C., whear they had a skirmish & was Killed during the skirmish which they had with the enemy, but the 24th completely routed the enemy.

June 9th, 1862
Camp Near River Trent, N.C.

Drilling still going on reguler in our Camp. A steamer arrived—the Jersey Blue, [The] News of the 6th [June] stating Richmond still remains Rebel. Lieut. Bast [QM] received news today of the death of his Granmother [grandmother].

June 10th, 1862
Camp Near Trent River, N.C.

Lieut. Col. Sigfried had the Reigment formed & Brought [it] up into a Hollow Square for the purpose of Reading the sentence of a Court Martial held at Hatteras Inlet. Jack Phillips of Compny F received three months at Fort Macon at hard Labour & Corporal Weaver of Co. G had his stripes publicly, Before the regt., taken from him.[57] The Steamer Massachusetts, which had left hear two days ago, returned again. Rumors in New Bern [are] that Richmond is in our possession.

June 11th, 1862
Camp Near River Trent, N.C.

Lieut. Col. Sigfried [is] still on Court Martial. Lieut. Bast [QM] removed his personal goods to his Quartermaster's tent, being he has it pitched. Major Nagle had the Regiment out this afternoon & Drilled it & done better than he did a few days ago, but it was very short.

June 12th, 1862
Camp Near River Trent, N.C.

The day was spent principly [principally] in Compny Drilling. A party Concluded to wait to one o'clock to view the total Eclipse & to pass time, they took a row in a boat & have a tow on the [surf?] laying aft. The starbert [starboard] side became the harbert [harbor] side, suddenly & frequently. The first Locomotive passed over the New Bridge which Burnside built over the Trent River, which was totally destroyed by the Rebels in the late battle of New Bern. She came from Beaufort, N.C.

June 13th, 1862
Camp Near River Trent, N.C.

Today, the Steamer Ellen S. Terry, bringing Isaac Lippman & [2nd] Lieutenant [Thomas J.] Fitzsimmons [C Co.] North, but Brought no news of any importance.[58] Gen. Nagle had a Brigade Drill this afternoon & Kept the Reigment out Very Little. We received a pair of Guidons for the Regment. Sergeant Johnson of my Compny was appointed as the Left Genrel Guide.

June 14th, 1862
Camp Near River Trent, N.C.

Nothing of importance in Camp. No drill in the afternoon. Cleaning up for inspection tomorrow. Steamer Ellen Terry went north today.

June 15th, 1862
Camp Near River Trent, N.C.

Weather very warm until 8 o'clock, when a heavy storm arose & the Lightning keep up a Continual flash which Lighted the whole Country around. Genrel Burnside arrived hear this afternoon.

June 16th, 1862
Camp Near River Trent, N.C.

Compny Drill in the morning. Major Nagle had Command of our regimental Drill in the afternoon. Col.

[Thomas G.] Stevenson of the 24th Mass. Regt., acting Brigadier Gen., had a Brigade Drill.[59] The Col. of the 23rd Mass. Regt. was today appointed provost Marshal, [with] Vice Capt. Messinger resigning on account of Sickness.[60]

June 17th
Camp Near River Trent, N.C.

Gen. Nagle had a Brigaid Drill & done very well. [2nd] Lieut. [John L.] Williams of Co. F received a severe reprimanding from [the] Lieut. Col. for being out of Camp without permission.[61]

June 18th, 1862
Camp Near River Trent, N.C.

Drilling was all the topic of the day & Drilling, skirmish, Compny Drills with the trumpet Call.

June 19th, 1862
Camp Near River Trent, N.C.

Received 10 days rashons today. This afternoon was intended to make a presentation to Gen. Burnside of a handsome sword from the State of Rhode Island & also to have a Genrel review of the troops of this department but, on account of a severe rain setting in, it was postponed until tomorrow at 4 P.M.

June 20th, 1862
Camp Near River Trent, N.C.

The 4 Compnys from Hatteras received thear endfield [Enfield] Rifles today. The Steamer Sparks arrived hear today from the north bringing some papers dated 16th. Brought no mail. This afternoon the presentation of the sword to Gen. Burnside by the state of Rhode Island took place. It was one of the finest Military Displays I ever witnessed. 16 Reigments participated with all thear transportation and Baggage trains. The Baggage train was under the Superintendence of the Divisions & under Command of [1st LT] Quartermaster [Theron E.] Hall [21st MA].[62] Gen. Burnside made a very neat speech & was very appropriate to the ocation [occasion].

June 21st, 1862
Camp Near River Trent, N.C.

Compny Drill this morning & no Drill in the afternoon, giving the men thear reguler time for tomorrow's inspection. A very large mail arrived hear by way of Beaufort by rail.

June 22nd, 1862
Camp Near River Trent, N.C.

The weather was very warm. After inspection, the Lieut. Col. had a small Battalion formed, who marched to town & heard a very good sermon preached by our Chaplin [chaplain]. Lieut. Bast [QM] and [William H.] Hardell [Hospital Steward] went to see an alligator that was Caught in the Neuse River.[63] Another mail arrived today.

June 23rd, 1862
Camp Near River Trent, N.C.

Having had some very poor rations issued to our men, we asked for a board of survey & it was granted & they Condemned 77 boxes of hard Bread & 500 lb. of Bacon & a lot of Beans & Hominy [as] unfit for use. The weather ws very warm all day.

June 24th, 1862
Camp Near River Trent

Today we war Drilling Compny Drill with the trumpet in a field of pretty long grass & it was very warm. I sounded the call of "lie down" & I told Lieut. Wood [B Co.]

[to] take the balance of the drill on this movement & the Call "to rise up" was sounded. The men said that was a Beautiful movement. A Compny of Rebel Cavalry made a dash into Morehead City last night Carrying off some 12 Niggers. Thear object was to destroy the rail road but [they] did not suckseed in thear enterprise. We had a heavy thunder storm today.

June 25th, 1862
Camp Near River Trent, N.C.

This morning at Reveille, after Roale, the Compny was all in line & did not appear to move off the ground. As usual, they hung Back & the officers, Lieut. Bast [QM] & Lieut. Wood [B Co.] & Myself, went in to to my tent & Shortly, the orderly Came in & said, "Captain, you are wanted on the Compny peraid ground," & I went over & I saw a box with a Brass plate on it and the orderly Sergeant [William H.] Hume [B Co.] opened the box, took out a Beautiful sword with a yellow scabert [scabbard] & solid Silver Bands & stepped in frunt of me & said, "Captain Wren, I have the pleasure of presenting this sword to you as a token of Respect from the members of Co. B, of which you have the Command, with the high appreciation of you as a man & an officer. Take it, Captain, as the gift from your own men."[64] I received it & with it, I was too full to say anything for a moment as I knew nothing of it & it was quite a surprise & took me entirely unprepared, but I thanked [them] for the honored gift, Coming from Soldiers in the field of actual service & I hope that it will neaver be dishonored by me. I felt proud of it. It was the first sword presented to any officer in the 48th Regt. Thear was quite a number [who] rushed on the Parade ground of Co. B when they saw me Coming out of my tent. They had some inclination of it & it was inspected by nearly all the officers of the Regment. It was made by Tiffany & Son & Cost 150 dols. in Boston.

June 26th, 1862
Camp Near River Trent

This morning I was informed by the Quartermaster that 18,000 rounds of Cartridges had bin sent to the 48th Regt. That looks a little like work. This evening thear was 2 Caissons Brought into [Camp] by some of the first division, who had a skirmish some distance out of town. Our Regt. Drew 4,000 round of Blank Cartridges.

June 27th, 1862
Camp Near River Trent, N.C.

Gen. Nagle had the Brigade out drilling this afternoon, Lieut. Gowen of Co. C, acting adigent, received a splendid horse today, [which was] turned over to him for [his] own use. Quartermaster Hall promised to get one for Quartermaster Bast & exchange [it] for his.

June 28th
Camp Near River Trent, N.C.

The Regt. practised firing all forenoon & fired Sixty rounds & done very well. The Captains received orders [as] to how many men they have [present] for heavy marching in thear respective Compnys prior to preparing to move. The Cossack and the Ellen S. Terry arrived hear from New York Bringing a mail.

June 29th, 1862
Camp Near River Trent

Lieut. Col. Sigfried ordered the Quartermaster to Draw seven days' rashons for the Reigment. Reguler marching orders was read on Dress perade. It is that each Regt. is to be ready to march in 8 hours' notice & Quartermaster Auman [G Co.] has furnished the schooner that the Brigade Baggage is to be put aboard.

June 30th, 1862
Camp Near River Trent

We had muster for pay this morning at 5 o'clock A.M.. The monthly review & inspection was dispensed with on account of the anticipated move. The program has bin changed for land to that of water.

July 1st, 1862
Camp Near River Trent, N.C.

[We] Received orders this day that the 48th Regt. will embark on board of the steam Transport, Cossack, at Day Break tomorrow morning, with 7 days' provisions on board by that time.

July 2nd, 1862
on Board steamer Cossack

Our Regt. struck tents this morning at day Break and Carried them on Board of the Baggage Schooner, after which they marched & embarked on board of the Steamer Patuxent, which Carried us down to the Cossack. By 8 o'clock A.M., [when] all the men [were] on board, the anchor was raised & the steamer proceeded to pick up two schooners—one loaded with horses & the other with soldiers of the 51st Regt. Pa. Vols. The whole expedition [is] Composed [of] a fleet of thirteen vessels—Six fine steamers & Seven schooners. When having one of the schooners in tow & [while] about fetching up the other, our steamer ran aground & the schooner ran into her Slightly and injured her by tearing away one of the Cranes and ripping up part of her upper deck. The schooner escaped without sustaining any injury whatever. At 10 A.M., we received orders to run down the river twenty-five miles & then Come to an anchor until tomorrow morning. After supper, Gen. Nagle Read an order to the officers, stating that he is to proceed with his Command to Fortress Monroe & there await further orders. This greatly relieved the minds of the officers as thear was Considrable [considerable] speculation as to our destination. The evening was passed very pleasantly on the aft deck by having the band playing and [by] the singing of songs by Lieut. [Henry P.] Owens of Co. D & Mr. [Edward L.] Haas [musician].[65] We had Considerable rain in the afternoon & a very heavy thunder storm prevailed and besides, the air was very Close & warm. All hands retired about 10 o'clock P.M.

July 3rd, 1862
On Board S. [Steam] T. [Transport] Cossack

Last night, the steamer Phoenix arrived with private dispatches to Gen. Nagle. This morning at Day Break, the fleet set sail again and arrived at the swash off Hatteras Inlet at 4 o'clock P.M. & Cast anchor. At the same time, the steamer Alice Price brought us news that Richmond had bin taken by our army & [it] gave orders for us to remain at anchor until further orders. After supper, the Officers held a meeting for the purpose of Celebrating the 4th of July in some suitable manner. Quartermaster Auman [G Co.] made a very neat & Spirited little speech. Lieut. Gowen [C Co.] & [QM] Sergeant [Jacob] Wagner went ashore on a tug.

July 4th, 1862
On Board of S. T. Cossack

This morning we war aroused by a steamer arriving alongside and giving us orders to return to New Bern again; so our steamer set to work amediatly [immediately] & weighed anchor & proceeded to pick up the schooners, which she had dumped before anchor was Cast Last evening. It was eight o'clock A.M. when we set sail for New Bern. Sergeant Wagner has bin Left behind. The Celebration for which arrangements had been Made last evening was dispensed with on account of being under way. All the vessels Comprising the fleet ware very gayly decorated with flags. It was 4 o'clock P.M. when we arrived at New Bern, after enjoying a very pleasant trip up the river. The masts presented a very fine appearance as every vessel had all her

Colours flying in honor of our birth day of our independence.
The steamer Landed at her Wharf at [the] Neuse River when
the Reigment Landed and marched direct to thear old Camp
ground on the other side of the Trent River. They pitched
thear tents again. The same evening a flag of truce arrived
in town Just as we arrived, bringing quite a Number of
Citizens who had Cleared out in the approach of our troops.
Lieut. Bast [QM] remained on board of the steamer all night.

July 5th
New Bern, N.C.

Lieut. Bast [QM] had Just got all the Commissary
stores off the boats when they received orders in Camp to
have all the Commissary stores Brought Back again & have
[a] full ten days' rashons on Board by daylight tomorrow
morning & the rasions was all on board by midnight.

July 6th
on Board S. T. Cossack

Struck tents at 2 ½ o'clock A.M. & took them down
on board of the Gilbert Green. At Break of day, our Regt.
marched to the wharf, whar they landed the other day, and
embarked on board of the steamer Cossack again at Precisely [precisely] 8 o'clock A.M. & got under way & steamed
down the river, whear we picked up the schooners, which
we took in tow. It was noon before we got fully under way
for Hatteras Inlet. [We] arrived off the swash at 11 o'clock
at night & dropped anchor on account of the Channel being
very difficult to navigate during the night. We enjoyed a
very pleasant trip down the river and through the Pamlico
Sound.

July 7th, 1862
on Board of S. T. Cossack

Off the swash at Hatteras Inlet, we weighed anchor
this morning at 5 o'clock A.M. [We] Let the schooner Phoenix

tight on the bar. When we went about 3 hundred yards ahead of the Phoenix, we run tight on the Bar. Our regiment disembarked & went on Board of the Phoenix & the Steamer Highland Light & [the] Phoenix ware both hitched on to the Cossack. Up to 9 o'clock, we had made but little headway, but we are now in tow of 2 Steamers. A lively Brease [breeze] of wind Arose at 9 o'clock A.M. & Carried the Schooners over the bar without towing. 2 of them has Just passed us & Looked Beautiful as they passed. The tug Boat Champion gave us a pull but did not get us off. Another schooner passes us. A Small Tug in Sight from the direction of New Bern Signalled to us Just as we got off of the Bar at ¼ past 12 o'clock Noon. 2 tugs with the Highland Light took us & put us on Board of the Cossack again & we proceeded to Hatteras Inlet & anchored at the Inlet. 2 steam tugs & the Highland Light went to the schooner Recruit, which had the 21st Mass. Regt. on board, to help them over the bar. At 3 o'clock P.M., orders [came] from Gen. Reno by steamer to take the schooner Recruit in tow & go to sea, which we did & [we] went out [of] the inlet heaving Considrable as the sea was rather rough. We saw the New Lights, in the evening, of the Hatteras Light house. They revolve every minute, which is a beautiful view. We did not see the Beacon light, as we passed it too early in the evening.

Virginia:
July 8–September 4, 1862

July 8th, 1862
On the Atlantic Ocean

This morning, the water is as Calm as the sound of Pamlico. Our steamer runs heavy & appears to be playing out, but we arrived at 2 o'clock P.M. & anchored opposite Fortress Monroe, whear we ware very glad to get out of the marine service, as we war well drilled in trimming ship & taking in & out the Larkert [larboard] & Starbert [starboard] Hasers [hausers]. The mens' Cooked rashons being out, we had the Cooks to go ashore & make [a] fire on the beach & Cook 2 days' rashons, which took them all night. I went ashore & had a Splendid Bath in the salt water near the Fortress & had a very good night's sleep.

July 9th, 1862
Fortress Monroe, [VA]

I took off our steamer, this morning, to the Hospital at Fortress Monroe, Corporal Johnston, Israel Eiler & John Heafling [B Co.]. Our Steamer took in Coal & water at the fort. Gen. Nagle Received orders to go up to Newport News & Disembark the troops & the steamer then [is] to anchor in the Stream. We reached Newport News at 8 o'clock P.M. & marched up to the Camp ground and Bunked on the grass. [We] had no tents. Being tired, we all slept sound during the night.

July 10th, 1862
Newport News

Received orders to pitch tents & be ready to march at an hour's notice. Busy all day pitching tents. I was officer of the day, which has bin the Case with me the Last 4 times we moved.

July 11th, 1862
Newport News

(We remained in this Camp until the 25th & during this time we war Drilling & preparing for the field.)

In the meantime, I sunk, for the Quartermaster of the post, a very fine well, down to the gravel bed. With my Compny being a great many miners in it, we went through the Quick Sand & had to four pole it, but our boys Completed it sucksessfully [successfully] & the Quartermaster paid us a very high Compliment in his report. At this point, Major Nagle resigned as Major & went home.

July 12th, 1862
Newport News

Our reigment went out on an expedition with one day's rashons in our haversacks. Started at seven o'clock in the morning with Cloudy weather & reached Young's Mill at one o'clock P.M. [We] Laid over to ½ past 5 o'clock P.M., when we resumed our march & reached Warwick Coart [Court] House at 7 o'clock P.M. & quarterd in a wheat field. Gen. Nagle Came over to our Compny & was talking very serious, as being in frunt of the enemy & I burst out [in]

Laftur [laughter] & I said, "We won't be hurt tonight," & he laughed & said, "Well, this little trip was Just to Break the men into marching. I thought we Could not do much on one days' rashons."

July 26th
Warwick Coart House

Across this morning & after Breakfast we Commenced our march to return to Newport News & arrived in Camp very tired, [it] being the first good march we had made on foot (& [we] remained in Camp until the second of August when we Break up Camp.)

August 2nd, 1862
Newport News

Struck tents at 5 o'clock A.M. & embarked on Board of the steamer Cossack, Bound for Fortress Monroe & [we] weighed anchor at 6 o'clock P.M. & dropped anchor opposite the Fortress.

August 3rd, 1862
Fortress Monroe, on Board of [the] steamer Cossack

At one o'clock this morning we weighed anchor & steered out for the Chesapeake Bay & shortly after getting under way thear was one of the men [who] shot himself, the ball going right through his Body. [With] the Ball, entering about the Navel and Coming out near the hip, he blead [bled] fearfully. It was a beautiful morning. After Day Break, we passed the mail Boat & thear was severel of our vessels in the fleet in view in the Chesapeake at 10 o'clock A.M. & at 8 o'clock A.M., we passed a ship in full sail. Being square Rigged, she Carried, in all, 14 Difrent [different] pieces of sail & a fair wind filling [her] sails & Causing a splendid appearance & a beautiful sight on the water. We anchored at 9 o'clock P.M. in the Potomac River.

August 4, 1862
on Board the Cossack in the Potomac River

[We] weighed anchor at 5 o'clock A.M. [We] proceeded up the river and, about 7 o'clock A.M. Mattis Shaeffer [D Co.], who shot himself last night, died & passed away very easy, having lost so much blood.[1] At 8 o'clock, we passed Port Tobacco. Theair are Beautiful scenery on the Potomac's Banks and Washington selected a home of much taste & in splendid scenes on both sides of the river. [The] Natural formations are the scenery of note. 2 o'clock P.M., we are just arriving at the Aquia Crik [creek] landing & is going on board of Cars and [we] arrived in frunt of Fredricksburg [Fredericksburg] & remained at Fredricksburg until the evening of the 12th of August.

August 12th, 1862
Camp Frunt of Fredricksburg

We left 4 of our men behind hear, sick: [Sgt.] Robert Campbell [B Co.] & Joseph Kirby [B Co.], Thomas Conell [B Co.] & [Samuel] Stanley [B Co.].[2] We left Camp this evening at 6 o'clock P.M. We started [the] march & Continued it until 3 o'clock in the morning of the 13th & took no nap until 6 o'clock A.M. & started again on the march & marched all day until the evening of the 13th & put up for the night and resumed our march again at reveille, which was at 4 o'clock in the morning of the 14th & reached the railroad station at 11 o'clock A.M. of the 14th, [which was] Leading to [Gen. John] Pope's army & we thear Cooked 2 days' rasions & then embarked on Board of [the] Cars of the Orange & Alexandria Railroad & disembarked at the Culpeper Coart House, 4 miles from the Battleground of the 9th. After being in our Camp, quite a number of the 46th Pennsylvania Regt, visited & gave us all the perticulers of thear Regment of the 9th engagement. They suffered severely. Thear was only 250 men, 3 Lieuts. & one Captain & theair Colnal, being the only field officer Left, Major [Joseph A.] Matthews [46th PA] of our Fort Washington was wounded in the arm

& [it] had to be amputated.³ [Gen. Irvin] McDowell [is] Considered to have acted very poor in not Bringing up his Command and [he] was only 4 miles from [Gen. Nathaniel P.] Banks when he was engaged with [Gen. Thomas J.] Jackson.⁴ Jackson would not believe that Banks was the only one that was fighting him. This information was received from prisoners taken. During the night, it rained very, very heavy & having no tents, it was rather Disagreeable.

August 15th, 1862
Camp at Culpeper C. House

Still raining. (We left Culpeper on the 16th for Cedar Run, [and] Slaughter's Mountain & encamped thear. We had no inspection thear.) On the 17th, being Sunday, today, [the] 2nd Meryland (Maryland) Reigment, 4 Companies of them, went out on picket & took one rebel Prisoner & one flag & one spy Glass & the implements of a Rebel signal Corps.

August 18th, 1862
Cedar Runs⁵

Had reguler inspection, according to the President's order. I had all my men accounted for Monday, August 18th, 1862 after which, we received orders to pack up and take 3 days' rashons in Haversacks. Sent all our Baggage trains away at 7 o'clock P.M. in the evening & the troops moved off at 12 o'clock P.M. on a forced march & marched until daylight & then took Breakfast. This was Tuesday morning of the 19th & marched all that day and reached the foard [ford] at Kelly's Bridge that evening & Camped thear that night. My Compny was Detailed to go on picket after arriving in Camp very tired but all went out and was stationed on the Rappahannock river & [were] extended up about 2 miles. The right of my Compny rests on Whitleysville Mill & running to Kelly's Foard and [the] Brigaid Connecting with [the] 2nd Division, under Command of Colnel [John]

Hartranft of [the] 51st P.V.[6] Nothing was seen or heard. All was Quiet along the line.

August 20th, 1862
Kelly's Foard

Still on picket. I changed the stations a little to have more advantage. At 9 o'clock A.M., Gen. Pope & Gen. McDowell & Staff & Bodyguard entered the extreme right of my Company line, us being the extreme out-post Picket.[7] I waited [on the] reception myself & had a little Conversation with Gen. Pope Concerning my outpost after which, they went down to Gen. Reno's headquarters. During the day, thear was quite a Number of Rebel Cavalrymen seen & they Came out & shot one of our Cavalry at Kelly's Ford— 5 Balls Lodging in him & [he] died in 3 or 4 hours afterwards. The Line of battle was then formed both by artillery and infantry & signal Lines formed. In the evening, we ware all ready for action. Ceverel Companies went out during the Day reconnoitering, but [they] did not fire a gun. The right wing of our Regt. was out under Command of Lieut. Col. Sigfried, but [they] did not discharge a gun. The artillery then threw 2 shells in the evening. We ware relieved of Picket at 5 o'clock in the evening of the 20th.[8]

August 21st, 1862
Kelly's Foard

The morning was Cloudy & [we] look for rain. Lieut. Wood went out to procure some provisions. A lively engagement with the Cavalry took place. One reigment of Cavalry engaged. On our side, the Battle still going on & one Battrey of artillery went out. Heavy Cannonading in [the] hearing of our line. At present, ½ past 2 o'clock P.M., I am detailed as Field officer of the day & is to take post at 4 o'clock P.M. Last night & this morning had the pickets on a sharp Look out, being the orders of Gen. Reno. At 11 o'clock P.M., 2 Cavalrymen came in to our line, brought in by the pickets stationed above Whitleysville Mill & they had no Countersign & they war ordered to Dismount & produce thear papers & they ware for Gen. Reno from Gen. Pope. They war bearers of dispatches & ware Conducted to Gen. Reno's head Quarters under a Cocked pistol by the field officer & guard & I delivered the papers to Gen. Reno in person. I dismounted the 2 Cavalrymen at 4 o'clock A.M. On the morning of the 22d of August, 1862 thear was a Commissioned officer & one Cavalryman Came into our lines from Pope's head Quarters with orders to Gen. Reno to Join Pope at the Rappahannock station & the whole Command was put in motion. At 6 o'clock, I was ordered to Draw in all the pickets as all the troops was on the march. This order I received from Reno in person. After drawing in all the pickets, we followed the troops & Caught up to them about 1 ½ hours afterwards. In the hurry, I forgot my army overcoat & did not think of it until we ware about 3 miles retreating from our former picket but Uncle Sam [was] too Late. We all arrived at the Rappahannock station at 11 o'clock A.M. and was thrown into Divisions & Stacked arms & received 50 lb. of Crackers to each Compny & at 4 o'clock P.M. we marched into and took posision in Line of Battle. The Line was formed as follows: the Line of Artillery [was] in front of the first Division under Comand of Gen. [Isaac] Stevens and in the rear of the artillery & [of] the 2nd Division, Commanded by Gen. Reno and in rear of the [Division] & each soldier in Line & at his post, we ware formed in [extended] order. It rained very heavy before Coming into the field and after Coming in line & [it] Rained During the night, which made it Quite disagreeable but all the men [were] in good Spirits as [General Franz] Sigel was driving the enemy from theair posision. The Battle [was] Commenced this morning by our Artillery & was responded to by the enemy & has bin keept [kept] up very lively ever since. The Battle was opened at 6 o'clock A.M. by our artillery. At 12 o'clock A.M., the Cannonading somewhat Ceased. Gen. Sigel got on the other side of the river.[9] Last night, the prisoners Just returned, Stating that they were Shelled out when building a Bridge to bring the sick & wounded

over, which is 150 in Number, but [they] have again returned to attempt it again. The rebels has sent a flag of
truce into our Line, but Gen. Pope will have nothing to do
with it & sent them Back. Our Reigment was moved 4 miles
to the right this morning & [it is] still on the march. The
Battle [is] still raging & ["Stonewall"] Jackson [is] trying
to get across the Rappahannock river but has not suckseeded
yet. One of his reigments got partly over but got Cut up
awful by our Artillery, having a masked Battrey & [it]
opened on them with great Loss to the enemy. We still
marched on until ½ past 12 o'clock at night when we Lay
down to raise up again at [the] Bugal [bugle] sound.

August 24th, 1862
Sulphur Springs

The Bugal sounded at 4 o'clock A.M. & [we] marched
until 10 o'clock A.M. & [we] shelled the valley near the river
& [we] formed line of Battle, but [received] no reply from
the enemy. We renewed our march and Just as we advanced,
the rebel guns replied & we fought our way up to the Sulphur
Springs. Just after the rebel Guns opened fire, theair Cavalry Came out on the opposite mountain about 100 Strong,
in the rear of our train & I, having Command of the train
guard and had some on picket, I Called in the Pickets &
formed the Compny in Line. The men Could see for themselves what they had to do as they [Rebels] ware in sight of
each other but they did not advance. So, they shelled us,
but fired too high. We reached Sulpher Springs in the evening at 8 o'clock P.M. & Lay down, very tired.

August 25th, 1862
Sulphur Springs

[I] Slept sound last night. Had a good night's rest.
Bugal Sounded at Sunrise for march & all in good trim,
having had good Coffee & plenty of it. Received orders to
return to Kelly's Ford & was marched by the town of Warrenton & as thear is an attack Contemplated, [we] was

formed into Line of Battle & Cooked Coffee for the men, at 2 o'clock P.M. Still in Line of Battle at ½ past 2 o'clock. Received orders to march to Warrenton Station or Junction & when within 2 miles of the Junction, we halted & Camped thear that night. Arriving at that point at 11 o'clock P.M., our Reigment was very much affected with the Long march. It being principly [principally] through the woods & a Dark Night, my Compny had 3 stragglers behind at the end of the march.

August 26th, 1862
2 Miles from Warrenton Junction

Bugal sounded for march at 6 o'clock A.M. & [we] Marched one mile on the other side of Warrenton Junction, whear we halted & Cooked three days' rashons. I applied for shoes and shelter tents. I had Cooked for my men a Large mess of Beans & fresh Beaf [beef], which they war much in need of. We got a night's rest, all being Quiet during the night. Hear, I made my Haversack into a Knapsack & it gave me a great Deal of ease in marching, having both shoulders for support.

August 27th, 1862
one Mile from Warrenton Junction

We started the march at Day light for Bethel, above Warrenton. We received News that Jackson had burnt one of the railroad Bridges, Cutting off our Supplies between Warrenton Junction & Alexandria. We Countermarched & pursued after him & got in his rear again. At 8 o'clock in the evening, we Camped at Greenwich Church, in the woods. It is a very fine place for a Country Church. We got a night's rest at this place.

August 28th, 1862
in Camp Near Greenwich Church

At 3 o'clock this morning, the 48th regt. was Brought into Line to go on the advance Picket. At 3 o'clock this morning, four Compnyes—A, B, I & D Joined reigment, as it passed. We had Coffee before [we] started [to] march & we heard that Jackson had reached Manassas Junction. Gen. Pope said, "We have him Bagged, if we Can only Keep him." We started at 6 o'clock for Manassas Gap. Cannonading [was] heard on our Left. Just after leaving Greenwich Church, whear we Camped last night, we finally arrived at Broad Crick [Creek] whear the Battle was fought on the 27th, whear one of Gen. Reno's Battryes [batteries] was engaged. It is 2 ½ miles from the Manassas Gap. We leave this place at 11 o'clock A.M. Jackson [is] supposed to be 3 or 4 miles ahead of us. We are pressing him hard. We arrived at Manassas Junction at 1 o'clock P.M. & found that Jackson had Left yesterday after setting fire to our railroad train & Destroying its Contents—Being army supplies. The Cars was still Burning & some Beaf was in part of the ruins & looked pretty well roasted & our men Cut some of it & eat it. Mike Divine [B Co.] of our Compny said Jackson wasn't the worst of men, that he Cooked rashons for us and Left.[10] The Charge on the train was made by Jackson's Cavalry and was made at Night. We are told theair was only 3 or 4 Compnies of our troops at this point when it was attacted. It is an awful sight to see the destroyed train. It is about a ½ a mile long. Our Compny roale was Called at Broad Crick & we found the following men Absent: Joseph Brooks, Thomas Conell, Thomas [C.] Littlehales, William [H.] Ward, George Marsden, Henry Copeland. We left Conell & [Sgt. John] Homer at Warrenton Junction on the 27th of august & also [Sgt.] William Kissinger went to the hospital thear.[11] We have not bin in tents since we Left Fredericksburg on August 12th. We had applied for Shelter tents. We arrived at Manassas Junction. We found the traces of all [the] Shelter tents all Burned up. At 3 o'clock P.M. of the 28th Thomas C. Littlehales arrived at Manassas & got into Camp with us & reports all of my men within 1 ½ miles of this Camp. Joseph Sefrin Just arrived at 4 o'clock P.M. & reports [Philip] Carlen & [Nicolas] Shiterhour Near Camp.[12] Homer & Kissinger Left the hospital at Warrenton Junction for Alexandria—Kissinger on the 26th [in the] A.M. & Homer on the

27th [in the] P.M. Carlen and Shiterhour Joined the ranks again at ½ past 4 o'clock P.M. of the 28th of August at Manassas Junction. Roal was Called & the following was absent: J. Brooks, H. Copeland, T. Conell, G. Marsden, W. Ward. We left Manassas Junction at ½ past 4 P.M. At 6 o'clock, Conell returned to the Compny. On the parapet walls of the fort near the Junction, we can see troops moving on the Bull Run Battle ground, supposed to be Jackson's. I had a splendid view of our Column & it Looks well. At ¼ past 6 o'clock P.M. of the 28th heavy Cannonading took place & we ware ordered into Line & after getting on [the] march, it Commenced to rain perfict torrents. I do not know that I ever saw it rain so hard in my life. For about ½ an hour after being on [the] march, we saw artillery that was engaged & Commenced on the old Manassas Battleground. We marched towards Centreville. It got Dark & then [we] encamped for the night. A little after dark, we Cooked Coffee & gave the men a half rashon of Fresh Beaf & then Lay down for the night.

August 29th, 1862
on march to Centreville

At 3 o'clock this morning I got awake with the Coald [cold] & I got up. The battle was opened at 6 ½ o'clock A.M. Our artillery [was] put on the right of the Line. Had a Compny roale Call this morning. Absent: J. Brooks, Marsden, Ward & Copeland [All B Co.]. Gen. Pope Just passed our line & he takes things quite Cool. He was smoking a Cigar when he passed. We marched to Centreville & when we arrived on the height, we flanked to the Left & moved on towards the Battle, which is going on. [We] supposed Jackson to be retreating & our troops [are] in his rear. 11 o'clock A.M.—hear we passed the rebels that was taken prisoner. Thear was between 4 & 5 hundred of them. Thear was some of them [who] fought against us in New Bern, North Carolina. Some of my men recognized them & they remarked that they would not fight anymore. Gen. Pope Just passed our Brigaid Line, the men being in the field resting, being very tired & hungry, but [having] no time to attend to eating. At present, our Cavalry [are] in the rear of Jackson's lines. After our artillery had silenced the rebel guns, the infantry line taking posision & now being in Posision, the Battle then had to be decided by the infantry. At 25 minutes past 2 o'clock P.M., our Brigade entered the Battle line & before we advanced one hundred yards, we received a volley of Musketry into us, but we keept our line well dressed & we advanced & fired about 20 minutes Direct to the frunt but [we] was not getting any further advanced, the rebels being in the old road Cut & we was ordered to Cease firing & then ordered to fix Baynet [bayonet] & we Charged the Cut & routed the enemy out of the Cut & we held the Cut & we war advancing beyond the Cut when a masked battrey opened & drove us Back into the Cut & while we war advancing beyond the Cut, our Left was unsupported & the enemy got around our left & got in our rear & we then had a fire to Contend against in frunt & rear. I went up on the Bank to see the movements of the enemy & I saw them, quite plain, Crossing the road on our left & in our rear & I told Gen. Nagle & he Could not believe it & the adjentent [adjutant] Bertolette, [who] was at our left & I went up on the Bank the second time & while up [there], my men Called at the top of thear Voices to, "Come down or you will be Cut to pieces."[13] I felt the rim of my old hat quaver [quiver] Like [a] Leaf. The adjtent [adjutant] & myself went & we told Nagle the enemy was in our rear & we received a heavy volley from the rear. Nagle then flanked the Regt. by a right flank on [the] Double Quick & [they] retreated, Leaving orders for Captain Wren to protect the Left of the Cut until the Reigment got out. I saw through the move in a flash— better to Lose a Piece of the Loaf than to Lose a whole one & seeing that the reigment was out, I then flanked my Compny to the right & gave the Command, "Double quick, march!" & we passed through [with] the rebels on [the] Right & Left of us & [we were] within speaking distance of each other. On our retreating through theas [these] lines, the rebels yelled out, "Stop, you Yankee sons of Bitches. You are our prisoners." But we did not stop & after we had all got out, Gen. Phil Kearny was rallying his Brigaid & they all rallied to the 48th Coulers [colors] & they & the 48th went in again but was over powered & driven Back.[14] During the rallying to the Colors, Gen. Phil Kearny, having but one arm & meeting some of his Brigaid said, with the Bridle rein between his teath [teeth] & his sword in his hand, "Come on and go in again, you sons of Bitches & I'll make Brigidear [brigadier] Genrels of every one of you." Darkenss Came on and the Battle ended for the day. During our retreating, I fell with my Breast striking a stump & I thought I was a prisoner sure when 2 of my men picked me up & helped me out & it made me very sick & we went a little to the side & they thought they would Cook a tin cup of Coffee for me & Just as we sat down, a solid shot buried itself right between us & [I] Said, "Boys, let us get out of this." We went up to whear thear was a group of Staff officers & I was relating our narrow escape when a solid shot Buried itself right between Gen. Pope & Gen. Reno, who was setting down together & they looked at each other in the face & said, "I guess we had better get away from hear" & they moved to the one side [to] another Seat. All Hostility Ceased for the night, both forces holding thear posisions. Pope [was] waiting anxiously for the arrival of Gen. Fitz John Porter, who was to have bin hear today, but at night [he] had not arrived yet.[15] I felt quite proud of my own Compny as they behaved well during the whole Battle & obeyed the Commands & stood true to thear work. So did our Regt. An old artilleryman who had gone [to] the Mexican War said [that] during the time that our Brigade was engaged, he neaver heard such a steady fire keep up for such a long time, of infantry, in his Life. From the time we went in, until we Came out, it was Just 1 ¾ hours. I looked at my watch as we went in and look at it when we Came out. We fought in a thick woods & the powder smoke hung [about] & we war all most as Black as Niggers, perticuly [particularly] around the mouth & eyes, when we Came out. During the Battle, 5 of my men was surrounded by rebels but was relieved by out troops again, and, at another time, 8 of them war taken prisoners & 3 of them was relieved by our troops. Paul Sheck

[B Co.], my old Cook, was in the hands of the Rebels, but was relieved by some of our men. The 3rd sergeant of our Compny, [John G. W.] Basler, had 2 plugs of tobacco in his Haversack & a Bullet went right through both of them & Private [Sebastian] Bickert had a Ball go through his Cartridge Box.[16] George Marsden, a rather slow soldier to move, saw a rebel up in a tree & he took aim on him & he fell to the ground like a log. The men said that act made up for all [of] George's lost motion, as a number of them saw the act. During the time we war advanced, one of our men, Nicolas Shiterhour, shot the Coler [color] Bearer of the enemy's Flag, but [he] got wounded afterwards. He was shot in the thigh. The Ball went right through but did not Break any Bones. The Rebel Troops that our Brigade drove out of the road Cut was the Lusiania [Louisiana] Tigers, which we fought at New Bern, North Carlina, March 14th. As we advanced to the Cut, they said, "Them is Burnside's troops. We know them by thear line & thear Charge." We, at night, lay under arms on the field whear we war Driven Back to & having unslung our Knapsacks & [we] had thrown them in a pile before we went into battle. This ground became the Center of the 2 Armies & thearfore, we were deprived of all our Knapsacks & Blankets. We thought it hard to have no tents but hear we had neather [neither] tents nor Blankets, the enemy Capturing All.[17]

August 30th, 1862 on Bull Run Battle Field

This morning, being after the Battle of yesterday—[the] 29th—I had Compny Roale Call & the following was the List of killed, wounded & missing of Compny B of the 48th Regt. of Penna. Vols.:

1. Louis M. Reece, Private—Killed
2. 2nd Sergeant Thomas Johnson—wounded in head
3. 3rd Sergeant J. G. Basler—wounded in leg
4. Henry T. Copeland—wounded in leg & arm
5. Samuel Stanley—wounded in hand

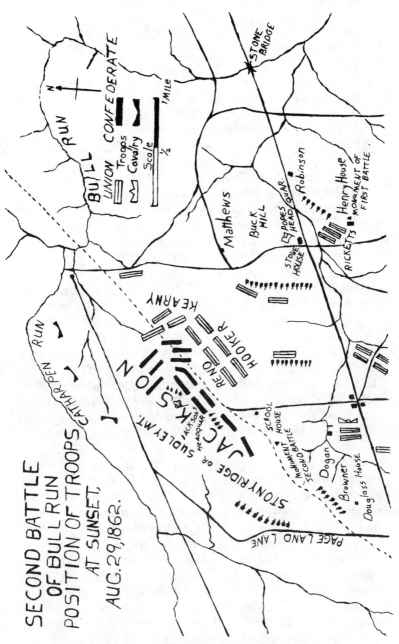

SECOND BATTLE OF BULL RUN
POSITION OF TROOPS
AT SUNSET,
AUG. 29, 1862.

Drawn by Matt Pfister from
Battles and Leaders of the Civil War

6. Thomas G. Williams—Spent Ball in Shoulder
7. William Hill—wounded in Head
8. Corporal Joseph Kirby—spent Ball in hand
9. John Lucid—wounded in hand, Slightly
10. John Heafling—in Back, spent Ball
11. [Sgt.] Sebastian Bickert—in Back, spent Ball
12. Nicolas Shiterhour—wounded in thigh
13. Sergeant Philip Hughes—taken Prisoner
14. Corporal Jacob Freshley—taken Prisoner
15. John Evans, Private—taken Prisoner
16. Joseph Rarig, Private—taken Prisoner
17. William Bradley, Private—taken Prisoner
18. George W. Johnson, Drummer—taken Prisoner
19. [Cpl.] George Evans—wounded in the Leg[18]

Amediately after roale Call, Lucid & Kirby returned from the Hospital & I found my list of wounded to be Correct up to this time, being 11 o'clock A.M. At 1/2 past 3 o'clock P.M., the Battle was resumed & was very heavy on our left, when Reno's Battrey took posision on the Left of his Command & the 48th Regt. [was] ordered to support the battrey & our Reigment was moved by the left flank, which brought me with, my Compny, leading the line & we went in Double Quick. As the Grape from the enemy's guns was very thick & Close to us and on our march [to the] Battrey, acaisoneley [occasionally] a shell would burst & we naturally Ducked our heads. Lieut. Col. Sigfried, being alongside of me directing the Line of march, remarked & Said, "Captain, you are very Complimentary today." "Rather," so said I, "and I notice you don't neglect to return the Compliment," & we had a good Laugh iver [over] it afterwards. We ware both Ducking. Our Battrey was fearfully attacted 3 diffrent [different] times & [it] was well manned by the detachment that was working [it]. They Charged thear guns with Double Charges of Grape & sent the enemy Back with fearful slaughter. I was Laying Right in the rear of one of the guns with my Compny & Could see the effect plainly & it appeared as if they [the rebels] advanced in Close Column en Masse as the third Charge. The men fell on top of the other

& Just at this moment, Gen. McDowell gave way & Broak the Line on our left & Came & took posision in Reno's line with his whole Command. Amongst them was the 13th U.S. Infantry. Genrel Reno, finding that McDowell had made an opening in our line, moved [his] troops to the Left & Sigel, who was now on the Left of Reno, moved his troops to Reno's Right & they Closed the opening that McDowell had made & held the posision until Dark. Our Battrey keept firing until [the] Darkness of the night Caused both armies to Cease. Fitz John Porter [did] not yet Come nor tidings of him near. After Dark, I was ordered out with my Compny to form a skirmish line, by Gen. Nagle, in frunt of our Brigade, with orders to advance & find out what the enemy was doing & then Come back & report [that] which [they were doing]. "Gen.," said I, "we Cannot form a skirmish Line in this thicket of woods & in this dark night. The men will fire on each other in the darkness. The only way I can see to form this line for the safety of the men is to form a single file & feale [feel] each other." "Well," said Nagle, "use your own Judgment," So I formed my Compny in [a] single rank & each man felt the other by a touch of each other & in single file, on a right flank, we advanced about ¼ of a mile when we could see the enemy all around thear Camp fires, which was very small ones & they ware as tired of the day's work as we war. I returned to our line & reported that the enemy was all Quiet & around thear Camp fires & in about half an hour, our whole Brigade retreated & fell Back to Centreville, [with] Genrel Reno's Division Covering the retreat until they came to whear Sigel had halted to rest & Cook Coffee. Reno passed Sigel & Sigel then Covered the retreat to Centreville. We halted hear & the dutchmen of Sigel's Command was very warm towards us. They asked whear we war engaged today & we told them we had helped Sigel to Close the gap that McDowell had made between Reno & Sigel. "O, my gott, you fight mitt Sigel; you Drink mitt me." & it was hear that the exclamation originated. Sigel's Mule Battries done good service in the Pope Campaign & they war well handled by the germans. Our men [were] almost worn out. They lay down alongside of the road

[by] 2 and three—in groups—given out. We Crossed the Bull Run Crick about 2 o'clock A.M. of the 31st & our trains passed over the Bridge & also our artillery & all being on a retreat, we had to wade the foard & it Just Took me up to the arms in depth & I neaver felt such Coald water in my life. Wet Clothing made our marching much heavier, but it had to be done. I had a poor opinion of McDowell as I understood the posision of our lines at the Bull Run Battle Line of the 30th. It was as follows: Reno [was] on our right wing & Sigel on our Left & McDowell in the Center. If McDowell had to give way & fall Back, which he did, [he should have] Come in the rear of Reno's Command. If Reno & Sigel had bin unsucksessful in getting through, then Reno alone would be Captured. In my estimation, it looked like traitorisom [traitorism]. [On] the morning of the 31st, Jackson's forces Came near our lines at Centreville, when out Brigade was ordered to the right & took posision & was relieved by night by another Brigade. All was Quiet during the [night]. My Compny was under the Command of Lieut. Wood [B Co.], as I was not well & was not on duty, which is the first day I have bin off Duty since I came into the service.

September 1st, 1862
Centreville

Our Regt. was in a field in [the] rear of the Line that they held the Day previous & went into Camp expecting to be withdrawn from the field [for] a day or 2 in order to recruit ourselves, but we found that our train was likely to be attacted & we war ordered into Line & about 3 miles from Centreville, we drove the rebel Pickets [in] & we ware fired upon when the Lines was formed & the Battle of Chantily was fought. The Battle Commenced at ½ past 5 o'clock P.M. & lasted until dark at night. It was an awful rally of infantry. The first division, Commanded by Gen. [Isaac] Stevens advanced thear line of skirmishers & Shortly afterwards was fired upon by the enemy.[19] The engagement became genrel & our (Nagle's) Brigade got into posision & [the] Brigade & all was engaged at the same time & the result was to us a victory, we holding the field & [were] shelled beyond the battleground until 9 o'clock P.M., but [we were] sorry when we heard [of] Gen. Stevens being Killed by a Ball going through his Brain. He was thought a great deal of by his men & we also lost another Brave & Good Gen., Gen. Phil Kearny. It rained fearful during the battle. After dark we Could not see each other. We fired at & for the flash of each others guns. I talked with Gen. Stevens Just about 20 minutes before he was shot. He passed through the line at my Compny, [he] being on a road which the Line Crossed. On the morning of the 2nd of September, about 2 o'clock A.M., we started the march for Fairfax Court House. In the march, the Mud was very deep, owing to the rain & the army trains & troops passing over it & on the march Sergeant Nelson [W.] Major of our Compny lost one of his shoos [shoes], [it] having stuck in the mud & thear was no such thing as to stop to look for it.[20] The orders war "go ahead" & when I found it out, I informed the men of the Compny to be on the look out & pick up an old shoe as we passed some of the old Camps & when we arrived at Fairfax Court House I asked Major if he had got a shoe yet & [he] sid [said], "Yes." "How does it fit?" said I. "Just rait [right]." "What number is it?" & he held out his foot & said, "By Jesus, I think it is No. 16!" It was about 1 ½ inches longer then [than] the other one but it fit fust [first] rate. We rested hear a little & then resumed our march & [when] within 3 miles of Alexandria, we encamped theair for the night & had Capt. William Wren & [Lieutenant] Martin Coho [both of B. Co., 129th PA] to Call upon me & I was very glad to see them[21]. [I] ask them if they had heard from home lately & Martin Coho gave some important information regarding our Business at home. We camped hear all night.

September 3rd, 1862
Camp Near Alexandria

Still in Camp. All Quiet on the line of the army. Our teams with [the] Baggage has Just arrived, but no tents at all [were] Brought along. [It is] 4 o'clock P.M. Gen. Nagle

Just informs us that we will be moved from this place to-morrow whear we will be better attended to & recruit our-selves.

September 4th, 1862
Camp Near Alexandria

Remained in Camp until 8 o'clock A.M. & received orders to march over the Long Bridge & [we] marched through Alexandria & at night, we marched through Washington City & encamped on the other side of the Capital & at arriving thear, the men was tired & all hands [are] worn out. (This ends the Pope campaign & I firmly believe the Battle of 2nd Bull Run was lost by Gen. Fitz John Porter failing to Come up, as he Could have done in the same manner as Gen. Reno did from Fredricksburg to Kelly's Ford & up to the present, his march would not make ½ the number of miles nor any worse roads then Reno had to join Pope and I sustain the finding of the Coart Martial in finding him guilty. [This is with me] having bin an Eye witness on the grounds & a pertisipent [participant] in marching over the Country of which we fought & [we] Lost the Battle of 2nd Bull Run, which we Commenced August 12th, 1862 & [which] ended September 5th, being 24 days under Pope.)

Lieutenant Daniel Flagler
(Officers of the Army and Navy)

Colonel Clark Moulton Avery
33rd North Carolina Volunteers
(Clark, North Carolina Regiments)

Lieutenant Colonel Joshua Sigfried
48th Pennsylvania Volunteers
(The 48th in the War)

Captain Henry Pleasants
C Company
48th Pennsylvania Volunteers
(The 48th in the War)

Captain Oliver C. Bosbyshell
G Company
48th Pennsylvania Volunteers
(The 48th in the War)

Lieutenant Jacob Douty
K Company
48th Pennsylvania Volunteers
(The 48th in the War)

Captain James Wren
B Company
48th Pennsylvania Volunteers
(The 48th in the War)

Major General Ambrose Burnside
(USAMHI, MOLLUS Collection)

Lieutenant George W. Gowen
C Company
48th Pennsylvania Volunteers
(The 48th in the War)

Captain Joseph A. Gilmour
H Company
48th Pennsylvania Volunteers
(The 48th in the War)

Colonel John Hartranft
51st New York Volunteers
(Officers of the Army and Navy)

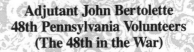

Adjutant John Bertolette
48th Pennsylvania Volunteers
(The 48th in the War)

Major General Philip Kearny
(USAMHI, MOLLUS Collection)

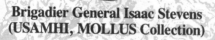

Brigadier General Isaac Stevens
(USAMHI, MOLLUS Collection)

Brigadier General Samuel Sturgis
(USAMHI, MOLLUS Collection)

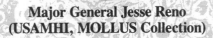

Major General Jesse Reno
(USAMHI, MOLLUS Collection)

Brigadier General James Nagle
(USAMHI, MOLLUS Collection)

Major Daniel Nagle
48th Pennsylvania Volunteers
(The 48th in the War)

Captain Joseph H. Hoskings
F Company
48th Pennsylvania Volunteers
(The 48th in the War)

Captain James Wren
Later in Life
(The First Defenders)

Maryland:
September 5–October 28, 1862

September 5th, 1862
Near the National Capitol, D.C.

In Camp in Washington City, we had a great many visitors today to see Reno's division & we looked very bad, being Lousey, Dirty & Almost naked & worn out. Gen. Burnside Came into Camp today & the Chears [cheers] he got was immense & the old Gen. had his Check shirt on, as usual, but the appearance of his troops appeared to effect [affect] him & [it] Could be plainly seen by thoes [those] who Knew him. Our prisoners that was taken in the battle of the 29th of August was released on perole [parole] & has gone to Annapolis until they [can] be exchanged. I took my Boots off this morning for the first time in 15 days & when when I pulled them off, it took bark off the frunt of my feet & they Blead [bled] & was very painful for a little while.

September 6th, 1862
Near the National Capitol, D.C.

I went into the City this morning to purchase some things for Lieut. Wood [B Co.] & myself & theair was a great many troops peraiding [parading] in & through the streets. I met Mr. Nathan Evans & John Winstall from Pottsville. [Thomas] Littlehales returned to our Compny today, being a prisoner of the 29th [of August] & reports Louis Reece Killed & [Henry] Copeland & [Nicolas] Shiterhour in the hospital in Washington and also a list of the wounded & prisoners of our Compny, of which we have & [it] is Correct according to his report.

September, 7th, 1862
Camp near the Capitol, D.C.

Sunday. I felt like seeing our men that was in the hospital & Left Camp & went to Carson Hospital on Union Hill & in the 27th ward, I found Henry Copeland of our Compny wounded in the Leg and Arm & also Abraham Klechner of Compny E. belonging to Captain [William] Winlack's Compny of our Regt.[1] He had his arm taken off but they are both in good spirits & appeared to be reconciled to thear fates. I gave them all the tobacco I had & gave them a dollar in money & expected to visit them again. I returned to Camp & found that our Regt. had marching orders to proceed to Leesboro, [which is] 8 miles from the City of Washington & arrived at our destination at 6 o'clock P.M., [with] the march, being very warm & Dusty. We met quite a number of persons that we Knew—Mrs. Evans & J. H. Lamb, of Pottsville & Mr. Carter of Temaque & Ceverel others & [I] was glad to see them, being from home.

September 8th, 1862

This morning we received our Dog Tents & received orders to resume our march. At 5 o'clock A.M., on the morning of the 9th, we ware put on light marching orders—only

4 teams to 10 Companies. I felt a little weak from the effects of the Diarear [diarrhea], but [I] packed up my little traps before I went to bed, which was 11 o'clock P.M.

September 9th, 1862
Camp Leesboro, [MD]

[We] left Camp at 6 o'clock A.M. & Left on the sick List Corporal [Joseph] Kirby & [Matthew] Hume, [Dominick] Burk, [John S.] Barnhart, [Thomas] Taylor & [William] Harris [all B Co.] [2] At ½ past 9 o'clock, we received orders from Gen. [Samuel] Sturgis, who Commands our division, that the Captains of Companies would be held responsible for theair Commands & ware not allowed to go into any Fruit or gardens. Gen. Sturgis passed our line at 10 o'clock A.M.[3] He is rather a portly man. He has the appearance of Capt. Belger of the 4th Rhoad [Rhode] Island Battry. We arrived at Brookville at 12 o'clock A.M. and Camped thear until the morning of the 10th [as] was our orders. When we Broak Ranks, the Lieut. Col., Sigfried, Called the officers in frunt & [he] was very angry & treated the Line officers with a good deal of Disrespect in the Language he used to the Commanders of the Compnies in regard to Keeping the men in the Column. The men Laying down on the road side & had given out & good men had done it from perfict Fatigue. [We] Received orders to move at daylight tomorrow morning.

Brookville
September 10th, 1862

[We] Received orders this morning at 5 o'clock to remain in this Camp until further orders. [We] received a mail & had 9 letters handed to me—one from George W. Johnson, our Drummer that was taken prisoner, stating that Sergeant [Philip D.] Hughes, Corporal [Jacob] Freshley, William Bradley & John Evans [all B Co.] was peroled & was at Annapolis. I sent on the 5 disemptive roals to Annapolis. I also received the Directions of William Davidson, Dominick

Burk, Thomas Taylor [all B Co.].[4] They are in Howard Hospital in 7th St. Conean's Place, Washington, D.C. I also received a letter from Corporal [Joseph] Johnston [B Co.], who has bin sick since the 8th of July. We left him at Fortress Monroe on our arrival from New Bern, North Carlina & also Israel Eiler [B Co.].[5] They are in Long Island College Hospital, New York, Brookland [Brooklyn]. He states that Eiler died on the 28th of July. He lay in the bed next to him. He died with the Typhoid feaver [fever], the same trouble Johnston has. I wrote to Johnston & gave him our directions. I also received official notice of the Death of Abraham Forrer [B Co.].[6] He died on the night of the 7th. His family was notified of his Death by the officers of the Hospital.

September 11, 1862
Camp Brookville

[We] Left Camp at ½ past 6 o'clock A.M. We passed some very fine residences on the road, being all private families. The Ladies ware very pleasant & kind to us & it made us feal [feel] as if we are near home, owing to the Kindness of theas [these] Ladies to the soldiers. We Continued our march & went a few miles beyond Damascus, making our march for the day 13 miles for the day. We got into Camp about 6 o'clock P.M. Lieut. Wood [B Co.] [is] still on the sick List, in the ambulance wagon. I made Coffee for Wood & myself & [it] having rained during the night, we got our Blankets all wet. [I] felt first rate myself. [We are] Leaving Damascus.

September 12th, 1862
Damascus, Md.

[We] left Camp at 1/2 past 7 o'clock A.M. Lieut. Wood [B Co.] [is] something Better. He is with us today & on entring [entering] the town of New Market, a very fine young lady, in Compny with 3 others, stood on the Bank of the railroad, [and] waved a Beautiful New flag of the Stripes & Stars & with a beautiful Bow of Ribbons of read [red], white & blue on the top of the flag staff. Our Company, as they passed her, gave three Chears [cheers] & the tiger. New Market is a fine little town. We halted theair for some time. The rebels was hear last night. They have Burnt the Bridge down 7 miles from hear. They have with them some artillery & have them in Posision on the other side of the Burnt Bridge. Thear is a prospect of a Battle shortly. Our artillery has passed on to [the] right of our Column & Genrel Reno has Just passed us with his Body guard—also to the right, ¼ past one o'clock. I just had the pleasure of shaking hands with my old Friend of Fort Washington, Lieut. [John] Edwards, [Jr.]—then—but now a Captain Commanding a Light field Battrey [Batteries L and M, 3rd U.S. Artillery].[7] The rebels [are] in sight & is within 2 ½ miles of Fredrick [Frederick] City & ware drove from the Monocacy Stone Bridge, which they had Commenced to Drill in the stone work to blow it up but was drove [off] by our troops & we Captured 2 pieces of artillery from them. They Left & we Camped on that ground tonight—the 12th.

September 13, 1862
Monocacy Bridge

I slept very well Last night. Lieut. Wood [B Co.] [is] very unwell & went to the ambulance wagon again. This morning thear is heavy Cannonading on the other side of Fredrick City. I went up to a high point in Company with Lieutenant [George] Gowen of Co. C & with my glass saw boath [both] armies Cannonading on separate mountains. [I] received orders to inspect the mens' Clothing & what they wanted in that line. The engagment of Artillery opened at 7 o'clock A.M. this morning & Continued until 10 o'clock A.M. with Considrable Liveliness. The rebels occupied the highest point of ground but our men done well. They drove the Confederates to the top of the mountain & Drove them through Middletown, taking quite a number of Prisoners. We marched within ¼ of a mile of Middletown & then camped for the night. From the Monocacy Bridge to Middletown is about 13 miles. The Monocacy Bridge is Built entirely of stone with 3 arches, making the span & the grass grows Green all along the track on top of it. At 10 o'clock P.M., we went into Camp at Middletown.

September 14th, 1862
Camp Near Middletown

Received orders to make fires & Cook fresh Meat at 5 o'clock A.M. for the 3rd time since we left Fredricksburg—August 12th, 1862. The Cannonading Commenced this morning towards the Town Called Hagerstown. It was very lively until 10 o'clock A.M., when we received orders to pack up & be ready for march in a moment's notice. I visited the hospital of our troops this morning & the Ladies of Middletown was very Kind to our wounded. Thear was only 7 of them in the hospital. The rest had not arrived from the field yet. The Cannonading Ceased at present. Our troops [are] in motion up South Mountain. At 2 ½ o'clock P.M., our Brigade was ordered up to the Battle field. At 4 o'clock P.M., we war in line of Battle & got in under heavy fire & had a Battrey being put in posision but before our Battrey opened, a rebel Battrey opened on our Brigade & [it] was nearly being a serious affair with our Brigade & our Battrey opened fire and dismounted the rebel gun & we saw them retreat with the gun, Dragging it on the ground & as they were retreating our Battrey fired on them agin & Killed one of theair horses that was retreating with the Disabled gun and the Battrymen got grait [great] praise & Chears from the troops and they well deserve it. It was as fine [an] action as Could be done with a gun. Quite a scene was witnessed by one of our troop's [in] action. Thear was a solid Ball fired at us from the enemy & it struck short & roaled along the field & [it] appeared to be almost stopped when one of our Soldiers ran afrunt of it and put his foot square on it & it tossed him head over heals [heels]. He done it in a Joke but it was serious to him as he was so severely Jarred that he had to be taken to the Hospital. At 5 o'clock P.M., I was ordered to the frunt with my Compny to form a line of skirmishers with the 51st New York in frunt of thear Brigade & we war

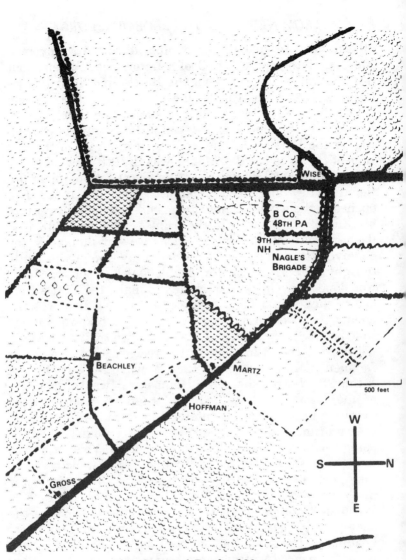

Original Draft of Map
Showing the Position of
B Company, 48th PA at Wise's Field
near Fox'x Gap, South Mountain, MD
(from forthcoming book by John Michael Priest
on the Maryland Campaign)

all extended in splendid order and advanced & my men [were] perfetley [perfectly] Cool & Determined. When about [in] 150 yards advance from the Battle line, in frunt, we meet the enemy's skirmish Line & we opened fire on them & they opened on us & theair ammunition reaching the Battle line, the old troops lay Quiet, Knowing the Contest was in the Line of skirmishers, but in the rear of the 2nd Line of troops in the Battle Line was the 9th Newhamshier [New Hampshire] Reigment & they [had] not bin under fire Before. They amagined [imagined] that the battle had opened & the whole reigment opened fire & fired direct into my line of skirmishers in the frunt & [the] 2nd Bull Run flashed right into my mind, whear we war flanked & the enemy getting in our rear. I ordered my Compny to "rally to right & Left from Center, double-Quick to the rear" & it was done very Quick as I wanted to make the Battle Line before they Could Load & fire again on us. If it was the enemy that was in our rear, better to be taken prisoners than be all Slaughtered & if it was our own troops, we would not receive thear 2nd volley. We reached the Line of our reigment & Lay Down with them & when all was Quieted & this 9th Newhansher [New Hampshire] [was] ordered out of line, I was asked by Lieut. Col. Sigfried to advance the skirmish Line again & I entered the skirmish Line again, the 2nd time, [with] all eyes then being on our Compny & being Company B of the 48th Reigment Pa. Vols., it was so understood that no firing under any Circumstances was to take place in frunt until we returned. So Company B was in the eyes of all the troops. So we advanced in Line of skirmish & got out in the woods about 125 yards & met the enemy's skirmish Line & we opened fire on them & fell Back, Loading at the same time & the enemy yelled & followed us up & we faced & stood again & gave them another Volley & being within 75 or 80 yards of our Battle Line, I ordered the Compny to "rally to the right & Left, double-Quick to the rear," which was done very Quick & we took our posision on the Left of our reigment in the battle Line. I reported to Lieut. Col. Sigfried that the enemy was within 75 yards of us, Coming up in the woods in frunt of us & that the 51st

New York skirmishers is also driven in & while I was de-
livering the Condition of things to Sigfried, the rebel flag
made its appearance & [they were] yelling, thinking that
they had got us on a retreat, when the whole Brigaid opened
fire from the Battle Line. Our Reigment remained in the
Battle until they had expended all theair ammunition & we
fell Back & the 2nd Meryland relieved us, they being in the
2nd line of Battle. The Line of troops was 3 lines deep—all
Laying down.[8] We then rested in a Corn field. [We] had
nothing to eat & was not allowed to build a fire, being in
range of the enemy. It was very Cold & I then had roale
Call and we found Alfred E. Bendley, John Howells, Johnathan Leffler [all B Co.] missing.[9] We would have suffered
severely from the 9th Newhamshier regt., while skirmishing, but theair range was about 5 feet too high, but when
thear ammunition reached us, it Dropped the Branches off
the trees down on us like the falling of wheat before the
scythe. In this Battle I Captured a large pile of knapsacks
belonging to the enemy & found in the knapsacks all Kinds
of Little articles, such as razors, photegrafs [photographs],
Bibles, with some very fine mottoes on the margins of them.
I put a Bible in my Pocket & had the men to Change thear
shirts & stockings & drawers. Being all in them in the shape
of Clothing, I had it done in 6 or 8 squads for fear we would
be Driven away while undressing & Changing & to our great
Surprise in this pile of Knapsacks we found a number of the
48th Regt. Pa. Vols. in amongst them, which was Captured
from us at 2nd Bull Run on the 29th of August & the men
preserved them & they felt good & said, "Now we are even
with the Johnnys in [the] capturing of Knapsacks."

September 15th, 1862
South Mountain Battlefield

Burnside permitted the troops to view the Battlefield they fought on yesterday, being the first time, he said,
the effects of a field after [a] Battle done no good to troops,
but this being a victory for them, he would grant them the
privilege, as they had erend [earned] it Like soldiers, and

we all went over & took a view & we found [that] in frunt [of] whear our reigment was engaged the enemy lay very thick on the field. I measured the ground & [in] 40 feet square I counted 16 of the enemy lying dead on it. We also found a number of wounded & we gave them water & Covered them with thear Blankets & Just to the right of my skirmish line of yesterday war two Cross roads in the shape of an "X" & on our frunt thear was a stone fence & behind that fence & in the "X" road the enemy lay very thick. One rebel, in Crossing the fence was Killed in the act & his Clothing Caught & he was hanging on the fence. Theas [these] ware the finest set of Rebel soldiers I ever saw, both in Muscle & in equipage. They wore fine gray uniforms. Amongst the soldiers that viewed the field was Captain Pleasants' [C Co.] Servent [servant], an Irishman, [William] "Billy" Fitzpatrick [C Co.] by name & when he returned, the Captain said, "Well, Billy, did you see them?"[10] "O, trouth I did," said Billy. "But, Captain," said he, "Isn't them [strange (?)] men?" "Why?" said the Captain. "Be my soul, every man of them has a third eye in his head." The Captain laughed & explained the matter to Billy & said, "Billy, you saw that stone fence?" "Yes, sir." "Well, the enemy was behind it when we war engaged yesterday & in order to fire on us they had to take aim over the stone fence & Consequently, they got shot by our men somewhear between the shoulders & head & that is the reason so many of them is shot in the head." Finding one of my men lying wounded, I detailed 2 men to assist him to the Hospital. This morning after viewing the field, we was Drawn up in line of Battle on the same ground we fought on last night & yesterday & was informed of the sad news of the death of Gen. Reno, who was wounded last night when we was engaged. He was wounded in the Lungs. He was in the rear of our Brigade at the time, Commanding & getting up a Battrey into posision when he fell. [There is] much sorrow amongst Burnside's troops as he was well liked & especially in the 2nd Division, which he Commanded & led in many Battles. He was a brave & wise Genrel & died without a murmur. All he said when Dying [was], "Tell General Burnside I have done all I Can for my Country" & when his Dying words was Convaid [conveyed] to the 2nd Division of the 9th Army Corps, it was then that the tears of Sorrow & tears of Joy mingled together and dropped from the eyes of his soldiers— in sorrow to Know they had lost a brave Commander & in Joy that a soldier had fell who loved his Country which they fought under. We heard today that Genril [General Joseph] Hooker had taken one thousand prisoners & the enemy [is] retreating.[11] He having Done good work in the field that he had Command of & he following up the retreating enemy, we heard today of the death of brave Major [Lewis J.] Martin of the 96th Regt. of Pa. Vols., [with] whom we war well acquainted & we very sorry to hear [of] it.[12] At this place, being the top of South Mountain, the Hospital was an awful sight, being a little house, by itself, & in the yard thear was 3 or 4 Large tables in it & as the soldiers was put on it (that was wounded), the surgical Corps Came along & the head of the Corps had in his hand a piece of White Chalk & he marked the place whear the Limb was to be Cut off & Right behind him was the line of surgeons with thear instruments & [they] proceeded to amputate & in Looking around in the yard, I saw a Beautiful, plump arm Laying [there], which Drew my attention & in looking a Little [at] it, and seeing another of the same kind, I picked them up & Laid them together & found that they are a right [arm] & one a Left Arm, which Convinced me that they war off the one man & you Could see many legs Laying in the yard with the shoes & stockings on—not taken off when amputated & in a field to the Left of this house was a long line of dead Soldiers Laying side by side with a Little inscription on thear breasts, giving thear Names & thear Compny & Regt. & the state they ware from & the pionear [pioneer] or ambulance Corps [was] engaged [in] digging a long trench, 7 feet wide to bury them in, which makes the [men] feal desperate towards the rebels, as many of them had brave Comrades who stood in Line with them was now taking thear posision in their Last Line.

September 16, 1862
Antietam Valley

The cannonading Commences very early this morning. We Could see the men at the rebel Battreys moving to & fro but [there] was not Light enough to see anything plain, [it] being too early in the morning, but after daylight, they opened fire on our reigment & shelled us out of our Camp, which we was in during the night. The dog tents never was taken down so quick in our reigment. We moved to a place of shelter. The artillery was engaged about 4 hours & resulted in our troops Capturing some [of the] enemy's artillery. The artillery done splendid at this point. They dropped a shell right in to a Rebel ammunition wagon & Blew it up & we Could see the whole thing go up in the air & our troops Cheared for over a mile in Lenth [length] of our line. The supply trains was all sent to the rear & we had no rashons but was ordered to go into a Corn field & a potato patch which was Close by & to supply from that. We thought it was hard, but we thought it was all right. This afternoon, I saw 2 mules, that the Driver said, that as they war marching along, a solid shot of a Cannon went right through the 2 mules, being a level shot. Gen. Burnside [was] in our Brigade Line & said he Knew of us being out of Rashons but he felt proud to inform us that we ware the advance of our army & we should only Bear with him until tomorrow, and he would relieve us with another Brigade to take the advance. We gave him 3 Chears & the Tigar [Tiger]. As usual, our army today drove the enemy all along the Line. The pickets war all Lively engaged until 8 o'clock at night. I was out with my Compny about 4 o'clock in the afternoon. [We] advanced about 1 ½ miles from the Bridge on the north side of the South Mountain & while thear a Staff officer came up to me and asked me if I had seen anything of note & I told nothing except of Mounted men on the opposite side of Antetam [Antietam] Crick & I directed [him] to the place & he took out his Large field glass & looked at them & he said, "Captain, that is Gen. Jackson & his staff." We know him by his Cream Colerd [Colored] horse & they have a map [and are] looking at it. Jackson is Dismounted one from the other but [we] saw them plainly Looking at the map. My own little glass only Could discern a man or a Battry or any object of the size about one mile but this was about 1 ½ miles from us. We returned to the regt. & we find the Lines of Battle drawn up with heavy forces on both sides. We [were] holding the Center line of Battle at 8 o'clock P.M.

September 17th, 1862
Battle of Anttetan [Antietam] Bridge

At ½ past 6 o'clock A.M., our division was ordered to take the advance & opened a reguler engagement under Command of Gen. Sturgis, who acted splendid in handling his troops. We drove the enemy from thear entrenchments & Barricades after 3 hours of a heavy Musketry engagement. The reigments engaged at the entrance of the Bridge was the 2nd Meryland, 6th Newhamshier [New Hampshire] & 9th New Hamshier, 48th Pennsylvania & 51st Pennsylvania. It was a Desperate struggle who should have Controal [Control] of the entrance & [we were] firing diret [direct] into the rebel Barricades at the Butment [abutment] the Bridge & during the struggle one of the 6th Newhamshir [New Hampshire] men Came to me & said he had got his finger shot off, but he did not want to go the rear, and he had about 40 rounds of Cartridges in his Cartridge Box. Then I said, "Well, it's victory or death hear." Thear is no moving or Commanding to be done hear as all the troops was working & firing into the Bridge & its Barricades. Said I, "Now you bite the ends off theas Cartridges & I will fire them Cartridges of yours," & I lay down my sword & took up the musket & I fired his musket until it got so hot in the Barrel I Could not hold it & [I] laid it down & by this time thear was plenty of spare guns & I picked up another & fired [it] until the Command was given to Cease firing. We then Charged the Bridge & Carried it & drove the enemy before us under a heavy fire of grape and shell from the enemy, but under it we formed line of Battle, but we suffered severely. I was then ordered to form a skirmish line with my Compny & advance & to Cover the anteatan [Antietam] Crick on my left & also the crest of the hill on the right. I advanced with my Compny & found the ground widning [widening] & I sent back for another Compny & Gen. Sturgis said, "Yes, let the men go at once," & then Capt. Winlack, with Company E, Came out & I Commanded the line of Both Companys & still the ground widened & I sent in for another Compny & Nagle Hesitated & he Consulted Sturgis & Sturgis said, "By all means, send another Compny," then Captain Bosbyshell Came out with Co. G. I then thought that a field officer would Come out & take the Command of the Battalion, but Captain Kauffman [A Co.] did not Come, he being the acting Major. So, I had Command of the three Compnys & when they war all extended & advancing, Gen. Sturgis asked who was Commanding that skirmish Line & Nagle said it was Captain Wren & he said he had not seen as fine a skirmish line since the war began & Sigfried remarked to Sturgis, "That is the same Captain Wren that was on the skirmish line at south mountain when the 9th Newhamshiar [New Hampshire] fired on him while [he was] out in frunt & after things got all Quieted with the 9th Newhanshir, [New Hampshire] he went out the 2nd time & he drew the enemy Back to the Battle Line splendid, without any Confusion, to us in the Battle Line. As he drew the enemy right up to our line, driving him he Came in on right & Left of our reigment on a Double Quick & took his posision in Line & reported the enemy within 75 yards, advancing in the woods in our frunt & I saw thear line & we opened fire on them." With theas 3 Companies, we advance until we met our own troops that had Crossed the crick 2 miles Below & they enquired of me who was Commanding us & they reported back to thear Commander & he ordered us to return to Gen. Sturgis & say that they had crossed the Crick 2 miles Below and that the lines was all right. So I Closed the ranks & drew in the skirmishers & returned to the Line of Battle of Gen. Sturgis & when I returned, I was met by Gen. Nagle & he was very angry with me for Coming Back without orders. I told him I had not done that & left him in his anger & went & reported to Gen. Sturgis, as I was instructed & the Gen. thanked me & said we deserved great praise for our well established skirmish Line & Gen. Nagle, after finding what our orders ware, Came to me & apologized & said he thought I had Come in without orders & also when you're out that way, you must use your own Judgement. I told him I understood that, although he acted very imprudent. While we war out on this skirmish line, we Came to a hay stack whear the enemy laid thear wounded on & when they retreated, did not get them away & during the time of the enemy leaving & our reaching it, the poor fellows was roasted alive. When we reached it, thear was some of them hanging with thear Legs over & thear Bodies still on the stack. We took them all out & laid them away from the stack & proceeded with our advance line skirmishing. I Captured 2 rebel officers' [swords] on this march. One of them Bears the following inscription, "Lieutenant J. W. Shoemaker, 4th Reigment, P.R.V.C., 33rd Reigment P.V." [13] This sword was Captured by the enemy from Lieut. Shoemaker at the 2nd Battle of Bull Run & is recaptured by Captain Wren's skirmish Line at the Battle of Antetam [Antietam] Bridge, September 17th, 1862. The other sword was a plain Line officer's sword with no inscription on it. Rashons being very scarce, [David] "Dye" Davis of our Co., seeing a rebel soldier's Haversack, Rather large, overhauled it & found it full of Johnny Cakes & emptied them into his & was eating them, when one of our men said he Could not eat anything out of a dead man's haversack & Dye replied, "Damn 'em man, the Johnny is dead, but the Johnnycakes is no Dead" & he Continued eating ahead.[14] We also saw a rebel Colnal [William R. Holmes, 2nd GA] who was Killed Laying in a ditch, who told Jackson he would hold the Bridge or Die in the ditch, as we was informed by a prisoner that was taken at the Bridge & Shoare [sure] enough, he died in a ditch.[15] He was in full uniform & had a fine gold watch which one of our troops relieved him of & a good pair of Boots which was taken possession of by 2 or our troops, each man a boot. They then tossed up who should have boath [both]. Captain Gilmour, of Co. H of our reigment, got a shoulder knot & the Buttons off his Coat was all Cut off by the men as relics of the event. Before Charging the Bridge, I Came near losing my life with 3 difrent musket Balls Coming right over whear I was firing with the musket & the men said, "Captain they have range on you," & watched Closly & saw a Soldier on the other side of the Crick, alongside of the Bridge, step to the one side from behind a tree & fire & the Bullet whistled over my head & [I] secured a safe place & had my gun at a rest & lined [up] for the tree & when he Came out to fire again, I fired but was too slow & I loaded again & Kept my gun lined on the tree & Just as he moved I drew tricker [trigger] & I saw him Double up at the root of the tree & that Ball Ceased Coming over my head. I made up my mind that if ever we ware sucksessfull to gain the Bridge & get on the other side, I would go to that tree & see if thear was any one theair & afterwards, in being sucksessfull in Carrying the Bridge & being ordered to skirmish, at once I went to this tree & sure enough, thear was a soldier laying thear & my men said, "Captain, that is your man," & [I] did think I had Killed one man in the Battle of the Bridge. Thear was a tree with 2 of our Cannon balls sticking in it & I thought that we ought to have Cut it down sent it home. It would only [have] taken about 5 feet off the trunk, as that space held both Balls. In the afternoon, we was again Drew up in Line to support the 51st [PA], Col. Hartranft, on our right until theair ammunition run out, when we took the frunt & suffered from the enemy's grape which Came fiercely on our reigment. We war Laying down & firing and along the road that run up the mountain, my men Lay in the wagon track but [it] was not enough protection, & Fred Knittle, Matthew Humes, Laurentis Moyer was severely wounded.[16] At 12 o'clock at night, we war all driven Back to [the] edge of the anteatam Crick & if the enemy had followed up the retreat they Could slaughtred us, but Burnside received orders to hold the Bridge at all hazerts [hazards] & we done so. At one o'clock in the morning, an ammunition wagon Came with ammunition and we got a fresh supply & we formed Line again and held the Battle ground until the morning of the 18th, at daylight, when we was relieved & Received Cooked rashons which Burnside had Cooked in the rear & Brought up in teams & they Laid the Beaf on boards which they Brought with the teams, but the minute the men was relieved, they Lay down in the field & fell asleep, shortly afterwards, Burnside Came up & he saw his meat on the Boards in a pile & he saw the troops asleep, [and with] the tears in his eyes & said, "It is rest they want first."

September 18th, 1862
Battle of Antetam [Antietam] Bridge

This afternoon, we war ordered to the frunt & was ordered to form a skirmish Line in frunt of our line, which I did & we advanced to a Corn field whear we ware Compelled to take a stand & take all the protection we Could & while hear, John Robinson of our Compny was shot in the belly. He and his Comrade, Carey Heaton, saw 3 rebel pickets & he had shot 2 of them & told his Comrade Heaton that now he was going to take good aim this time to get the 3rd one & while in the act of Capping his piece, the enemy shot him & the Ball took afect [effect] inches below the Navel & we war all very sorry as John was a perticuler favorite in the whole Company & was a good & Brave soldier.[17] I had him Carried to the rear with my own men & and taken to the ambulance Corps & Since then, I have not heard from him. I had his Knapsack taken to the wagon to be Carried. At 11 o'clock, Just heard from John Robinson. He is still Living, but will not Live long, as Doctor Reber told me himself. He says he is wounded in the abdomen & that is almost death instantly. We are still in the skirmish Line & dare not go eather [either] Back or forward as the Corn field is the Contested ground—the enemy in one end of it & us in the other & dare not raise our heads, except hearing from the enemy musket. At ¼ past 12 o'clock, we have had another of my Compny Killed. He was shot dead. I seen him fall & all he said was, "Oh, I have got it now" & fell & he did not suffer much as he died instantly. We dare not go into to him as the enemy had range on that ground & we was very ancious [anxious] to get his Body & we suckseeded in getting it & I had it taken down to the Bridge & had it

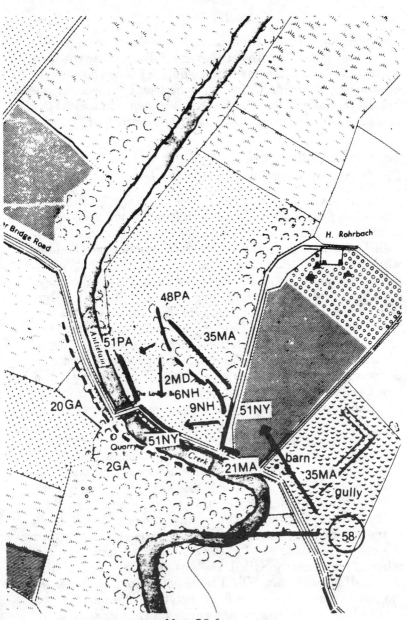

Map 58 from
Antietam: The Soldiers' Battle
by John Michael Priest

Buried in the field near the Bridge, whear we had the struggle for to get across. He was shot while in the frunt after taking water to a wounded soldier by Creaping [creeping] in the forough [furrow] to him & after he had given him the water, he begged on him to take him out & he belong to the 6 Newhanshier [New Hampshire], which Reigment & the 48th Regt. was warm friends & the distance he had to Carry him was not more than 100 yards & [Alexander] Prince Coult [could] not stand his pitiful request & got him on his Back & I don't think he made 4 or 5 steps with him until the enemy's Bullet hit him & he fell; through his kindness, he lost his own life.[18]

September 19th, 1862
Camp Near Antetam Bridge

This morning we are Camped alongside of the Battery that Alexander Prince's Brother is in. [Alexander Prince was killed the day before.] He told me he saw his Brother before he was Buried & I was glad he had seen him, even if he was dead. I gave him his pocket Book, which Contained $1.30 Cents in money & 3 rings & 5 Buttons which I gave to him & also the Bible, [which] he showed me a fiew [few] days ago & he got his Knapsack yesterday & he being his nearest friend, is entitled to it. I had John Robinson's Knapsack put in the wagon & is going to have it sent home to his father, Just as he had it packed when he was shot. We resumed march towards the Potomac & reached the Anteaton [Antietam] Iron Works at 5 o'clock P.M. & on arriving thear, we found that at daylight, the rebels had Crossed at daylight this morning at the foard, about 2 ½ miles down from us. A few Crossed over hear, some 2 or 3 Brigades. We Camped on the MD side of the river [on] the 19th & all was quiet, but 2 ½ [miles] below us, an Artillery engagement & also some infintry [were] engaged. We heard nothing of the enemy as they Kept Very Quiet, in ambush.

September 20th, 1862
Anteatam Iron Works

This morning we heard heavy Cannonading to our right & towards the Center. Nothing heard or seen hear. Our line's on the left & we got a rest all day hear. Today Lieut. Wood [B Co.] & Captain Kauffman [A Co.] Came into Camp in the ambulance wagon. Wood Still sick & unfit for duty, which makes me very much exhausted—having the whole Command of the Compny to attend to Myself, owing to my first Lieutenant Bast, acting Reigmental Quartermaster since we war in New Bern, North Carlina & my 2nd Lieut. being sick.

September 21st, 1862
Antetam Iron Works

This morning, I went down to a house & sat at a table at Breakfast for the first time for over 5 weaks [weeks]. The young Lady of the house Baked me 50 Biscuits & when I returned to Camp, I found theair was no orders to move and I had our dog tents pitched. We had Divine service hear, [which was] held by our Chaplain, Mr. [Samuel A.] Holman & [he] offered up a very fine Prayer. We gathered around him in the shade of a large straw stack. All [was] Quiet.

September 22nd
Antetiam [Antietam] Iron Works

I made out the following Descriptive roales & sent them off: Sergeant [Thomas] Johnson, Sergeant [John G. W.] Basler, Samuel Stanley, Henry Copeland, Joseph Rarig, Corporal [Joseph] Kirby & Frederick Knittle [all B Co.]. Corporal Kirby was sent to Locust Spring Hospital & Knittle was supposed to be thear also. William Ward & John Watkins [both B Co.] was detailed to relieve Philip Carlen & John Colihan [both B Co.] from the supply train, as they could not drive.[19] This morning, I was ordered under arms at 4 o'clock as the enemy was supposed to be Crossing the Patomik [Potomac] River.

September 23rd, 1862
Antetam Iron Works

Camp Rumors [have it] that Richmond & fort Darling was taken. [There were] reports that our Brigade is going to Washington but [they] turned out to be false reports. Lieut. Wood [B Co.] [is] still sick.

September 24th, 1862
Antetam Iron Works

I went & got a Couple of Chickens Cooked for Wood & Myself & also some Biscuits from the young lady [from] which I got them the other day. Captain William Wren [B Co.] of the 129th Regt. paid us a visit today & informs us that they have not bin in any engagements yet & feals like getting a try [at it]. All quiet in the Camp.

September 25th, 1862
Antetam Iron Works

Reveille [was] at day Break this morning. [We] received orders to pack up for [a] March. At 8 o'clock, [we were] still in Camp. I receive a letter from Louis M. Reece's [B Co.] Wife, whose husband was Killed at [the] 2nd Bull Run [in the] first day's fight. We struck tents at ½ past 12 A.M. for the march & afterward received orders to pitch tents again & [to] remain in this Camp for the night. John Cathers from St. Clair, belonging to the Pennsylvania Malishe [militia], paid us a visit and gave Quite an interesting account of the preparation of the Pennsylvania lines.[20] Being all formed, [they were] ready for the attack of the enemy when they made theair appearance in the state. Lieutenant Martin Coho, of the 129th Regt. [visited] & looks well. He says that they have bin on small rashons, owing to having no supply train, but is getting along Better Just now.

September 26th, 1862
Antetam Iron Works

Still in Camp; no orders to move at yet.

September 27th, 1862
Camp Antetam Iron Works

We remained in this camp a few days, when we took up the march into Pleasant Valley, whear we ware quartered in tents & our men received medical attention, being troubled severely of Direar [diarrhea] & was worn out from hard work & I was affected with it for the first time myself & I went to Dr. Reber & he gave me a dose & as old Mr. Struthers said, "It done it." I was to call up to the doctor next morning, but I did not see the doctor for 2 or 3 days after. When we met & [he] asked why I did not Come up & I told him, "You done it." He laughed & said, "Well, you had a good Dose." But, while in Camp in Pleasant Valley we all recruited & was in good trim in about 2 weaks [after] being thear. During our Camping in Pleasant Valley, Col. Sigfried had a leave of absence & Captain Pleasants was acting Lieut. Col. & Captain Kauffman [A Co.], Acting Major & the reigment required the [positions of] field officers to be filled owing to Col. Nagle having received his Commission as Brigadier Gen. & his Brother, Daniel Nagle, having resigned as Major on our return from New Bern, North Carlina, Leaving but one full Commissioned field officer with our reigment, Lieut. Co. Sigfried & in this Camp I received a letter from the Line officers of our Reigment, recommending me to Governor Curtin, for the rank of Major of the 48th Reigment of Pa. Vols. The officers of the reigment signed 2 recommendations. One they sent to the governor & the other they presented to me, which this is a copy of:

Camp Pleasant Valley Oct. 18th, 1862.
To His Excellency.
A. G. Curtin, Gov. of Penna.

We, the undersigned Commissioned officers of the 48th Regt. Penna. Vols., having the highest opinion of Captain James Wren of Co. B as a Military officer, do most Respectfully recommend him as a person in every respect Competent to fill the position of Major in this 48th Reigment as a tactician and a disciplinarian. He stands high in our estimation. His Bravery and Courage exhibited in the Late Battles of South Mountain and Antietam alone entitle him to promotion.

Names of officers & Rank of [the] same:
Capt. D. B. Kauffman, Co. A,
   48th Regt. Pa. Vols. Acting Major
Capt. Jas. Hoskings, Co. F,
   48th Regt. Pa. Vols.
Lieut. Henry James, Co. F,
   48th Regt. Pa. Vols.
Lieut. John L. Williams, Co. F,
   48th Regt. Pa. Vols.[21]
Capt. John R. Porter, Co. I,
   48th, Pa. Vols.
Capt. O. C. Bosbyshell, Co. G,
   48th Pa. Vols.
Lieut. Curtis Pollock, Co. G,
   48th Pa. Vols.
Lieut. Henry C. Jackson, Co. G,
   48th Pa. Vols.[22]
Lieut Jacob Douty, Co. K,
   48th Regt. Pa. Vols.
Lieut. Alex Brown, Co. H,
   48th Pa. Vols.
Lieut. Henry Boyer, Co. A,
   48th Pa Vols.
Lieut. Thomas Bohannan, Co. E,
   48th Pa. Vols.[23]
Lieut. I. F. Brannon, Co. K,
   48th Regt. Pa. Vols.
Capt. William Winlack, Co. E, 48th Pa. Vols.

Lieut. U. A. Bast, Co. B, 48th Pa. Vols.
Lieut. John Wood, Co. B, 48th Pa. Vols.

After receiving this, It made me feal very good, not for the office, but to know that I had the Confidence of my fellow officers & I felt Confident [that I] had the Confidence of my Company & I had all Confidence in them & was not afraid to take any position under any Circumstances with my Compny B, as they all proved true in Battle. During our stay in this Camp, thear was quite a number of persons [who] visited us from Schuylkill County, among whom was Gen. Nagle's Wife & Lieut. [William J.] Hinkle's [Co. H] Wife & the 2. Mr. Hellems from Schuylkill Heaven, John Bindley of Pottsville & My Brother, Thomas Wren of Pottsville.[24] I got an ambulance wagon & took them over the Antetam Battle ground & took them to the Antietam Bridge & showed them the spot whear our Reigment Fought on & they took some of the flat Bullets in theair pockets home with them. I sent the 2 swords I captured home with them.

Camp Pleasant Valley
Oct. 22nd, 1862

This morning our old friend, Mr. Joseph Bowen, of Pottsville arrived in Camp & was received very warmly. He brought with him all the Commissions of Promotion with him & of all those that ware promoted and with the others, a Commission for me as Major of the 48th Regt. Pa. Vols. & [it] was announced at Dress perad & [that I was] to be obeyed & Respected as such, by Capt. Pleasants, Commanding the 48th Regt. & [I] was ordered on duty as Major on the 23rd & had Command of the Regt. & at Dress peraid I had the order read of Lieut. Col. Pleasants as Lieut. Col. of the 48th Regt. Pa. Vols. & to be obeyed & respected as such & after Dress peraid, Lieut. Col. Pleasants invited all the officers of the Regt. to take a drink of Kindness with him tonight, which we did with a great deal of enjoyment.

Camp Pleasant Valley
Oct. 24th, 1862

Having bin put on duty as Major, I tendered the Command of Compny B of the 48th Regt. of Pa. Vols. to Captain Bast, who was promoted to the Captaincy & who was Relieved as Regimental Quartermaster of which he had served in since his appointment at New Bern, North Carlina, April, 1862. I then invited all the officers of the Regt. to Come & take a Drink with Major Wren this evening, in Kindness, but finding that the ammunition could not be got, I Countermanded the order, but [they were] to Keep themselves in readiness to move [at] a moment's notice, as I expected the supply train every moment, and I would move at once. The train arrived on the 25th & that evening & as old Fatsinger of Mauch Chunk said to the Washington Artillery, "Gentlemen, Face the enemy" & all appeared to enjoy themselves. The 2 Mr. Hellems & our old friend, Joseph Bowen, was with us & enjoyed it.

Camp Pleasant Valley
Oct. 26th, 1862

Today I sent notice to Captain Bast [B Co.] that I would treat my old Compny B this evening, If it was agreeable to him & his officers & I received a note stating that he would be pleased to see it & that he would join me as Captain & we would have a good jollification & we made all the preparations & met at Compny B's Quarters & everything went on spiritedly, but when we Come to say goodbye, it was harder to do then [than] we expected, but we finely [finally] parted by shaking hands. I impressed on the minds of the men to obey thear New Captain as I believed Captain Bast to be a good and an efficient officer & that I hoped they & the Captain would have [much] pleasure in the Compny together.

Pleasant Valley—Camp Near Sandy Hook October 25th, 1862

I turned over the following to Captain U. A. Bast [B Co.] of which [this] is his Receipt.

Camp Near Sandy Hook, Pleasant Valley

Received October 25th, 1862 of Captain James Wren, late Commander of Co. B, 48th Regt. Pa. Vols., the following arms & accoutrements:

51 Enfield Rifles
51 Cartridge Boxes & Belts
51 Bayonets & Scaberts [scabbards]
51 Body Plates
51 Gun Slings
40 Screw Drivers
 1 Gun Vice

U. A. Bast, Capt.
Co. B, 48th Regt. Pa. Vols.

Camp Near Sandy Hook, Pleasant Valley

Received October 25th, 1862 of Captain James Wren, late Commander of Co. B. 48th Regt. Pa. Vols., the following Camp & Garrison equipage, vis.:

5 Camp Kitls [kettles]
2 Mess pans
3 axes
1 hatchet
1 axe handle
1 Left Genrel Guide Flag
1 axe sling
53 shelter tents

U. A. Bast, Capt.
Compny B, 48th Regt. Pa. Vols.

Camp Near Sandy Hook, Pleasant Valley
October 25th, 1862

Received of Captain James Wren, late Captain of Co. B, 48th Regt. Pa. Vols., one Storm flag, which was presented to Compny B by the Citizens of Schuylkill County & [was] raised & floated on Fort Clark, North Carlina, January 1st, 1862.

U. A. Bast, Capt.
Co. B, 48th Regt. PA Vols.

Final Statement of Arms & accoutrements, Captain James Wren, Co. B, 48th Regt. Pa. Vols., Receipted to Lieut. Col. Sigfried for 83 Enfield Rifles & accoutrements.

Turned over to Capt. Bast at Camp Near Sandy Hook:	51
Expended in Engagements in 2nd Bull Run & Antietam:	26
Turned over at Falmouth for transportation:	6
Total:	83

This ending my Compny Commanding & [with Captain Bast] taking of the responsibility of Arms & accoutrements as Captain, I now devote my attention to [the] Business of my Reigment.

October 27th, 1862

Left Camp Pleasant Valley at 1 o'clock P.M. & Marched to Weaverton & then to Knoxville. From theair we took the [C & O Canal] Towpath and arrived at [New] Berlin [Brunswick] & crossed the pontoon Bridge & marched on towards Wheatland & at night Camped for the night. Our train not getting forward, we ware deprived of our tents & Blankets & theair being a white frost, we suffered with the Coald. The men's canteens got frozen tight with the water in them. We ware also short of provisions amongst the officers as thear mess Chest was in the teams with all theair provisions in them.

October 28th, 1862
Camp Near Berlin

Early this morning, Col. Sigfried & Quartermaster James Ellis Came into Camp & joined the Regt. again & after which we resumed our march toward Wheatland, Va., which we reached on the evening of the 28th & [we] remained in Wheatland until the morning of Nov. 1st, 1862.[25]

4

Virginia Again:
October 29–December 18, 1862

October 29th, 1862
Wheatland, Va.

In this Camp the field officers Combined to form one mess & all the servants ware to act as servants of the mess & thear was one officer to take Charge & I was again promoted & I excepted [accepted] the promotion as Kator [caterer] of the mess, with the understanding with the Col. that I should have an unlimited pass to go in & out of Camp as I pleased, in which he gave very willingly & being short of rashons, I was ordered on duty at once, but [I] was excused for today, but tomorrow, they would expect me to make a move with my Colered Brigade & Charge on some roast.

October 30th, 1862
Wheatland, Va.

This morning I started out of Camp & took with me my own Colerd servant, John York, and had him mounted on horse back with a Large Bag under him. We went out after provisions for the officers' mess. When we ware about 2 miles from Camp, we reached a farm house down in a hollow alongside of the main road. We entered & a lady waited [on the] Call & I told her we wanted to buy some provisions if she Could let us have them & she said that a Staff officer, belonging to Gen. Sturgis' staff, had bought all she had & he would Come with the servant & Bring them. [I asked], "He did not pay for them did he?" & she replied, "No, sir, he did not." "Well," said I, "that is our stuff. John, Buy them things. Well, madam," said I, "what is the price?" Well, the goose was so much & the Cabbage so much & the potatoes & Butter & ice & the other things, in all, she said, amounted to $6.25. "All right, madam, hear is your money. Hurry up, John. The staff officers will be waiting on us" & John got the Bag on the horse's Back & we started up the road towards Camp & about ½ a mile ahead of us, I saw an officer & 2 servants Coming down the road. I said to John, "John, we will take a short Cut through theas woods to Camp." "All right, Massa Major." So, in we went & John's Bag interfered in the Brush, but we got in far enough to let this officer & his 2 servants pass us un-noticed & I Countermanded the order of march & we struck out on the road & [I] told John, "Now we'll have to spur up," as we had lost time in the woods. "All right, Massa Major," and we arrived in Camp all Safe & when we dismounted, our Staff being all in a group, they asked John how we made out. "All right, sar. Massa Major fetch 'em Splendid. I was promoted while I was away on Genril Sturgis' Staff." Lieut. Col. Pleasants asked me about John's appointment & I told him we war on Gen. Sturgis' Staff [for] about 20 minutes & then relieved ourselves in the way Described & we had a good Laugh over it.

October 31st, 1862
Wheatland, Va.

Goose for dinner. We had him Cooked & invited one of Sturgis' staff to dine with us [with] whom we war well acquainted & he enjoyed the goose dinner but [there was] nothing said [about] how we got the goose & at the dinner table, he remarked [about] the fineness of the goose. "It was Delicious. We was to of had a goose or a turkey but when the Keator [caterer] went to fetch it, the woman said an aid [had] fetched it & we did not have any Goose nor turkey." (I begged our mess not to mention anything about our goose at the table as it might Create some trouble, but some 2 or 3 weaks afterwards, we war all in a tent & this same staff officer was present & the pleasantness of the officer was discussed. I remarked I was on Gen. Sturgis' Staff but I did not Like it & had myself relieved & he did not recollect of it & I told him the story of our Wheatland Goose & had a good Laugh. He thought I was good.)

November 1st, 1862
Wheatland, Va.

Left Camp about 10 o'clock A.M. & proceeded to Snicker's Gap. After arriving within 2 ½ miles of Snicker's Gap, we Camped for the night & pitched 2 of our marquees. The wind raised & blew very hard during the night. Cannonading was Kept up Late in the evening. Our troops Drove the enemy from theair mountain position. [Brigadier General Alfred] Pleasonton [is] still pressing [the enemy].[1] The enemy evacuated Snicker's Gap & Concentrated at a gap Lower down & will Likely Make a stand.

November 2nd, 1862

I had Command of the Picket guard of Gen. Sturgis' Division. [It consisted of] 170 rank & file, which after being drawn in, We Commenced our march to Join our Division, who had started 2 hours before us. We reached & Joined the Column about 7 o'clock at night. [The] picket guard, being out all night, was very tired when they reached the Column in Camp Near Bloomsville.

November 3rd, 1862
Camp Near Bloomsville

Left Camp at ½ past one o'clock P.M. & Counter-marched through Bloomsville [at] 5 minutes past 3 o'clock P.M. & Continued the march until we stopped & Camped Near Upperville at 8 o'clock P.M. During the night, the 2nd Brigade pickets war driven in & we ware all ordered into line of Battle. The men lay down with theair arms Loaded.

November 4th, 1862
Camp Near Upperville

This morning at 8 ½ o'clock A.M., [we] Reached in view of the town of Upperville & at 10 o'clock A.M., we reached Upperville & was drawn up in Divisions as ½ distance to await further orders. In the Lower end of Upperville is Ashby's Gap. Nothing of the enemy was seen thear, so we proceeded on to Green Garden & encamped theair for the night.

November 5th, 1862

Left Camp Green Garden. We resumed our march & Reached Camp Orlean & Camped theair for the night. It was Very rough ground we Camped on.

November 6th, 1862
Camp Orlean

About 3 o'clock P.M., we resumed our march towards Manassas, but taking the wrong road, we almost found ourselves in the Lines of the enemy through [the mistake of] Gen. Ferrero, "the New York dancing master", as the men Called him. It was an awful night. It snowed part of the march & then rained & it froze my horse's tail & [his] mane hung in Icicles & [they] rattled together. When the line was being reversed, it took sometime to turn the train & I was so Coald I was afraid to get off my horse, fearing I Could not get on again. I neaver suffered with Cold so in my life.

Finely [finally], we got on the right road & marched until 10 o'clock P.M. & Camped alongside of the road with the infantry in the woods & the artillery in an open field. It was so Cold in the field & they reported [it] to Sturgis & he ordered them to leave the guns guarded & Bring the men in the woods. Our reigmental officers, we all put our Blankets together & then put our oil Cloths under us & we all slept together & made out well under the Circumstances. The snow at daylight was about 2½ inches thick on us when we woke up, but the woods was a great Shelter to us during the night.

November 7th, 1862
Camp on the roadside

Resumed our march at 9 o'clock A.M. & marched to Waterloo & encamped theair for the night.

November 8th, 1862
Camp Waterloo

We examined the muster roales of the different Companies. All Quiet. Gen. [Orlando] Willcox Just passed our Quarters.[2] He [is] making his Quarters about 20 rods from our Regt., towards our right.

November 9th, 1862
Camp Waterloo

An order [has] bin received that Gen. Burnside has received Command of the forces in the field of the Army of the Pottomick [Potomac]. On receipt of the order, Gen. Sturgis issued an order requesting Divine services for the prosperity of Gen. Burnside & his Command, which was done by our Chaplin [chaplain], Mr. Holman. At 2 o'clock P.M., we received orders to march at once, which we did & Marched to Rind Mill & Crossed the Rappahannock about 4 o'clock P.M. & then passed through Amissville about 6 o'clock P.M. & encamped about one mile from that place, towards Culpeper.

November 10th, 1862
Camp Near Amisville

My little Horse, Billey, [is] sufring [suffering] very much from the scratches in his foot lock [fetlock] Joints. I had his feet washed out with hot water & Castile soap & [he] Looks much better. We received orders to march at once. The enemy [is] Close at hand. [It was] Quite an excitement to get the train. The troops fell back about ½ a mile & formed Line of Battle after which we advanced a skirmish Line with the 48th reigment to the support of Gen. Pleasonton's Cavalry. After a Considrable [considerable] engagement with the Artillery & Cavalry, the enemy fell back & at dusk in the evening we war ordered to Camp in a field, whear we war drawn up in line of Battle. The enemy threw Ceverel shells in the Center of our Camp (that we [had] left in the morning) shortly after we had Left it.

November 11th, 1862
Camp Near Amissville

This morning the sun rises very clear. Last night thear was a sharp frost & we, having no tents, we felt it. Very Coald. The men [have] run short of rashons owing to the supply train not getting up with the Supplies.

November 12th, 1862
Camp Near Amissville

We marched out of Camp at 5 o'clock A.M. Our teams started at 3 o'clock A.M. We fell back to Camp Waterloo & [we were] in the Camp all Comfortable when we received orders to march in 40 minutes, which we did & [we] marched to Sulphur Springs whear we ware 3 months ago, whear we war under [the] Command of our brave & and Good Gen. Reno & [we were] in Pope's Army. We encamped on a very rough piece of ground & yet, I slept well all night.

November 13th, 1862
Camp Sulphur Springs

I got up this morning well rested but the men still Cry out for theair Crackers, as they have not received anything since tusday [Tuesday] the 11th. After Breakfast, I visited the Sulphur Springs Buildings which at one time must have bin a very fine place. One of the buildings & the largest of 2 is burnt to the ground by our shell setting fire to them, [which happened] at the time, we ware hear before while in Pope's army. I recollect it well of seeing the heavy fire the night we arrived on the other side of the river. The building that is now hear is in good order, but all the furniture is taken out except a few bedstids [bedsteads]. Our Surgeons think of making a Hospital of it. I also Visited the Springs & found one of a square shape & Lined with marble & along side of it was a Large statue of a lady, but the anxiety of man is strong. They Knocked it to pieces, each one taking a piece. I Judge the statue Cost from 11 to 12 hundred dollars. The Springs are very strong with sulfer flavour. The taste of the water is similar [to] that of our Burning Mine water at Broad Mountain, Schuykill Co., Pa. Received orders to move into another Camp, which we did & rested for the night.

November 14th, 1862
Sulphur Springs

I got up this morning with the Coald but after washing & dressing I felt Very Comfortable as the morning was Very fine after sunrise. Reports [came in] from our pickets that the Major of the Provost Guard was taken prisoner. Our pickets was driven back at one time during the day, but we finally drove the enemy Back.

November 15th, 1862
Sulphur Springs

We left Sulphur Springs at sun rise this morning & marched Near Fayetteville. The enemy brought theair artillery into posision & opened fire on our train. We detailed one of our Battries & opened fire on the rebel Battrey & thear was Quite a lively engagement took place with the artillery. We had one man killed & 3 wounded. One of the wounded since died. They all belong to the Battrey.

November 16th, 1862
Camp Near Fayetteville

Received orders this morning to march towards Fredricksburg, Va. Our movement is rather slow. The 2nd Brigade [is] on the right. Today, weather being very fine for marching. Captain Gilmour [H Co.] arrived last night [at the] Camp Near Fayetteville & [had] no Drafted men with him. He brought my uniform & Saddle to Warrenton Junction. Nothing seen of the enemy. The railroad to Warrenton is to be abondoned after today.

November 17th, 1862
Camp 4 miles from W. Junction

4 miles from Warrenton Junction we received orders to pack up & be ready to march in 60 minutes towards Fredricksburg & proceeded on our march until within 18 miles of Fredricksburg & Camped theair for the night. Just as we had our tents up it Commenced to rain very fast but the rain being warm we did not suffer from it. The marching was very good today, as the roads was very fine. We marched in 3 Columns abreast of each other with the 2 infantry Columns on the Right & Left & the Artillery in the Center, which Looks well & Looks as if we ware going right into Richmond. I had all my New horse traps on today & works well.

November 18th, 1862
Camp 18 miles from Fredricksburg, VA.

We received orders to march at 6 o'clock A.M. It drizzled & Rained part of the day. We marched within 5 miles of Fredricksburg & Camped theair during the night. The marching was very good & Could have marched some distance farther but our orders was to Camp theair for the night.

November 19th, 1862
Camp 6 miles from Fredricksburg

I visited the side of the river & saw the enemy's Pickets on the side of the river. I saw the enemy in all grades Cavalry, Artillery, and Infantry pickets at the river. Thear is Quite an uproar in the town. People all moving out of it.

November 20th, 1862
Fredricksburg, Va.

I Visited the side of the river at the Lacey house & saw the enemy's Pickets on the other side. At ½ past 9 o'clock A.M., our Artillery opened fire from our Battries on the enemy & has fired 4 shots but no reply from the enemy. [Pvt.] Abe [Abraham] Nagle [D Co.] went home this morning, having bin discharged from the service for Disability.[3] The 4 guns fired this morning holds the railroad trains from going out of Fredricksburg to Richmond, Va. They attempted it twice, but it was no go. Our guns was too direct upon them. Arrival of the train with our Pontoon bridge to Cross the Rappahannock, opposite the town of Fredricksburg. They ware unloaded at 2 o'clock P.M. I purchased a very fine supply of rashons for our mess today from [the] Sutler. At 3 o'clock P.M., it rained very heavy but the teams is very lively at work getting the Pontoon bridge Fixture Delivered to the river Bank. Capt. [John R.] Porter [I Co., is the] CO. I was detailed to Picket Duty along the river opposite the Town. All is Quiet betwixt the 2 armies.

November 21st, 1862
Fredricksburg, Va.

It rained all last night. Rather cold this morning. Our pickets report having seen the enemy going through the streets in Regiments & theair Camp fires was about ½ a mile from town, 1 ¼ miles in Lenth Showing, Showing that they ware in good Force. Today a flag of truce was sent into town & Genrel [Marsena] Patrick was the provost Marshall, when we occupied the town on our first march at Fredricksburg under our brave Gen. Reno.[4] Lieut. Thomas Fitzsimmons [C Co.] tended his resignation today on account of Disability. It has bin very Disagreeable on account of it raining last night & partly all day. All Quiet. Our Brigade has moved about 2 miles from the river on account of the Low swampy ground. Our regiment [is] still supporting the Battrey that has direct range on the town & also the Depot Leading to Richmond, Va.

November 22nd, 1862
in Frunt of Fredricksburg, Va.

This morning, the rebel flag of truce Came into our lines & the reply that they received from Gen. Burnside was that our army would give the Rebs 16 hours to take all the Women and Children out of the town & also remove all the sick, as the Gen. Commanding intended to shell the town. This being Saturday & the 16 hours running into Sunday, it was posponed until Monday morning.

Sunday, November 23rd, 1862
Frunt of Fredricksburg, Va.

This morning everything Quiet. 2 rebel prisoners was taken past our Quarters up to Gen. Sumner's head Quarters. They gave themselves up. They are from North Carlina. Lieut. Fitzsimmons [C Co.] went home, he getting a Discharge for Disability. He took 3 letters home for me. We had inspection at 4 o'clock P.M. and it was very Cold while inspecting & again we got through. It was getting Dusk. After inspection of Arms, Lieut. Col. Pleasants [48th PA] & Myself inspected the men's Clothing & found that the men wanted Clothing badly for this season of the year.

November 24th, 1862
Frunt of Fredricksburg, Va.

It is a sharp Frost this morning. Col. Sigfried received orders from Gen. Willcox to put a guard on the building he formerly occupied on the bank of the river, opposite the town which is known as the Lacey house. The Col. also received orders to watch the movements of the enemy & report to Gen. Willcox every morning. The enemy threw up a new earth works Last night, having from it an enfilading range on us which is rather important to the enemy.

November 25th, 1862
in Frunt of Fredricksburg

White frost this morning. Rather Coald in tents. Our pickets Fired Last night about 8 P.M., Col. [Jacob G.] Frick, of the 129th Pa. Vols., paid us a visit yesterday afternoon.[5]

November 26th, 1862
in Frunt of Fredricksburg

Received orders to have inspection & review today by Gen. Sumner Commanding the Center grand division at 9 o'clock A.M. The Col. inspected the arms & awaited the Gen. to review us. At 12 o'clock, noon, we received orders that the review was postponed, after which I went to Falmouth to purchase some provisions for our Mess, everything being so high, I did not purchase much. Pottatas [Potatoes] was 4 dollars per Bushel.

November 17th, 1862
in Frunt of Fredricksburg

This morning, the weather is beautiful & Clear. Lieut. Wood [B Co.] & myself paid a visit to the 129th Regt. Pa. Vols. They Complained very much of not getting a full supply of rashions. I saw Captain William Wren & his 2nd

Lieut. [Jacob] Parvin, [B Co.] from St. Clair [PA], & his first Lieut. Martin Coho [B Co.] had gone up to our Regt. to visit us, but on our return to our Regt. we met Lieut. Coho on the road & had a good shake of the paw.[6] It was on the Bridge & the old Bridge fairly shook.

November 28th, 1862
frunt of Fredricksburg

This morning we had Regt. Drill at 10 o'clock A.M. & done very well. We had a visit of a french officer to view the rebel earth works. He belongs to Burnside's staff. The rebels is still throwing (sic) up earth work & redouts at various positions. We had Compny Drilling today with the Compnys of the regiment. We had the Locomotive to make her first trip today from Aquia Crick. She brought supplies for the army & she made 3 trips today. We had Dress parade in the evening of which I had the Command. We received orders to be ready to move tomorrow morning at 4 o'clock A.M. to Join our Brigade.

November 29th, 1862
in frunt of Fredricksburg

Got up early this morning to move up to Join our Brigade. We was relieved by the 8th Connecticut Regt. at Daylight this morning. We reached our Brigade at 10 o'clock A.M. & Quartered behind Gen. Nagle's headquarters. It is Very good Camping ground but rather small. All hands in Compnys went to work to arrange theair shelter tents. The field officers arranged theair tents. The field officers arranged theair tents behind Gen. Nagle's.

November 30th, 1862
Camp Near Falmouth, Va.

The men still fixing up theair quarters. Orders was read of Gen. Sumner taking up Command of the Right Grand Division of which the 9th Army Corps is a part. Inspection being the Last of the month, as usual, took place.

December 1st, 1862
Camp Near Falmouth, Va.

Still in progress in making our Quarters as Comfortable as possible.

December 2nd, 1862
Camp Near Falmouth, Va.

Received orders today to have Compny drills & also regimental Drills to make in all 4 hours a day & new troops to Drill 5 hours per day.

December 3rd, 1862
Near Falmouth, Va.

Compny Drill [was] this morning at 9 o'clock A.M. & Regimental Drill at 2 o'clock P.M. The Drilling of the regiment was very good & the Col. Complimented the Regt. very much for theair attention while Drilling.

December 4th, 1862
Camp Near Falmouth, Va.

All Quiet along the Line of the Rappahannock. This morning Gen. Sumner reviewed the troops of Gen. Fitz John Porter's old Command & others. Thear was a very large Turnout in the field. Col. Sigfried & Lieut. Col. Pleasants was at the review. I had Command of the Regt. [We] had Regimental drill in the afternoon & got along well.

December 5th, 1862
Near Falmouth, Va.

Regimental Drill, today, went Rather poor for the regiment. Thear must be more Caution on [the] part of [the] Compny officers—perticulery in passing the word of Command along the Line. I had Command of the Dress peraid this evening. Gen. Sturgis, in Compny with Gen. Nagle. Viewed the dress peraid & was highly pleased with it &

Sturgis inquired, "Who is that Commanding?" & Nagle replied, "that [he was] Major Wren—the Captain Wren that Commanded the skirmish Line at Antietam Bridge." Sturgis replied, "He Can Command a Regt." & Nagle replied, "Yes, Major Wren is a good officer."

December 6th, 1862
Near Falmouth, Va.

This morning, 75 teams of our division went off with 4 days' rashons. Paymaster Clark Came hear today & had the pay roales signed. He took supper with us.

Sunday, December 7th, 1862
Camp Near Falmouth, Va.

This morning we had inspection by the Compny Commanders, but being that I had 150 men on Picket, I was not present, being field officer of the day. We had the picket Lines extending to Falmouth on our right [and] Joining the 63rd Regt. Pa. Vols. & extending along the river about 2 ½ miles [and] Joining the 46th Regt. Pa. Vols. on our Left. I visited the guard at ½ past 9 o'clock P.M. It was very Coald. My Boots was frozen quite stiff on my feet by riding so far & stopping at each post to get the report from the Difrent [different] officers. When I reached Camp, I thought my ears was frozen. I visited the picket Line this morning, being the 8th & found all Quiet. The rebel pickets eyed me very sharp with a spy glass, I being mounted. I Judge the width of the river at this point [to be] not more than 2 hundred yards wide.

December 8th, 1862
Camp Near Falmouth, Va.

Received orders this morning to make the men's Quarters Comfortable, which leads us to believe that the winter Quarter is near at hand & for this purpose 2 days [of] Drilling was suspended & as my tent wanted some repairs, I had a Chimney built of small sticks of wood & then I plastered it with mud on the inside & also the outside & it answered very well.

December 9th, 1862
Camp Near Falmouth, Va.

Received orders today to inspect the men's ammunition & arms with great Care & to provide each man with 60 rounds of Cartridges. We found that the men's Clothing & shooes & stockings was very poor in Quite a number of the Compnys & had requisitions filled out by theair respective Captains for the required Clothing.

December 10th, 1862
Camp Near Falmouth, Va.

We had inspection this morning of the Arms & ammunition & found the Arms & ammunition in very good Condition with the exception of one or 2 Cases. Received orders to Cook three days' rashons & to be ready to move at a moment's notice. This is preparing for an onward movement. Received orders at 10 o'clock P.M. to march at 5 o'clock in the morning on the 11th.

December 11th, 1862
Camp Near Falmouth, Va.[7]

Moved out of Camp this morning with the intention of Crossing the river. We ware drawn up in line near Gen. Sumner's head Quarters. The artillery opened fire 10 minutes to 5 A.M. & continued firing very heavy until 9 o'clock A.M., when it Ceased to [allow the men to] Lay the pontoons, but the enemy's sharp shooters opened fire on our engineer Corps, Killing & wounding 60 of them. Our Battries then opened fire on the town & shelled it, setting fire to a large number of Buildings. The laying of the pontoons was suspended for a short time & the Artillery Continued to fire until 3 o'clock P.M., when our troops embarked in the pontoons & rowed themselves across. The troops that rowed across was the 7th Michigan Regt. They lost [in] Killed & wounded 40 men. The pontoons was then finished & reinforcements was sent over. The town was then skirmished & 50 prisoners was taken & Brought over to our Camp. Thear was Quite a brisk engagement [which] took place in the town Just at Dusk. The roar of Artillery was awful today. We had 140 pieces & [they were] firing on the town & [we had] 125 pieces to Cross with the infantry. Thear was 3 difrent Crossings—Hooker on the Right, [Edwin V.] Sumner in [the] Center, [William B.] Franklin [on the] Left.[8]

December 12th, 1862
Frunt of Fredricksburg, Va.

Our Division Crossed over on the pontoons this morning at ½ past 9 o'clock A.M. The enemy's Shot Came over our heads while we ware Crossing. After getting into town, it appeared that every building was riddled with shot & all the fences [were] Knocked down & very few of the inhabitants [were] in the town. Things in genrel looked bad in Appearance. In the afternoon, Hooker's Corps, on our right, Commenced to Cross the river & the enemy shelled them & they had to Cease Crossing for a time. The Cavalry Commenced to Cross & they war repulsed & had to wait & rested thair for the night. Our reigment, being near the Burnt Buildings, our men Clustered around the fire & one of the Chimneys fell & hurt one of Captain Winlack's men of Compny E of the 48th Regt. & during the night, another Chimney fell & Bruised William Hill of my old Compny B & at 2 o'clock in the morning of the 13th of December, he died from his wounds.[9] He was Bruised all over. His Leg was broken in 2 places. We buried him in the rear of the Baptist Church near whear we war Quartered in the town. I slept tonight in the Building of Mr. Wells who used to run the packet boat from Wilkes-Barre to the tunnel. He said he Carried Machinery for us when we war building & erecting our Collery at Wilkes-Barre. He knew me by some of the men of our reigment calling me by Name, "Major Wren."

He then Came up & said he knew me & I told him that my Brother, Thomas Wren, was the one he knew as "Tom", [who] attended to the Collery. I did not want to have much to say to him as he was rebel & we had Just Confiscated his boat & our government was using it on the river down near Aquia Crick.

December 13th, 1862
In Fredricksburg, Va.

[We] got out this morning at 5 o'clock A.M. & formed [a] line at 9 o'clock A.M. & at 12 o'clock noon, we advanced up through the town & after getting near the upper end of the town we then halted & at 2 o'clock P.M., [we] advanced & took posision in the Battle line & relieved the 21st Massachusetts Regt., Commanded by Col. [William] Clark.[10] We suffered Considrable in going into the Battle line owing to us having to Cross a plain, open field & right in range of the enemy guns. We war shelled fearfully. One shell dropped & exploded on the Left of our Regt., right between Lieut. [Henry C.] Jackson [G Co.] & myself [with] Jackson getting the gravel in his face & Neck.[11] We lost all [of] our ambulance Corps except 2 men. Richard Brown, belonging to my old Co. B, 48th [PA] Lost one arm & Michael Divine was Cut right in 2 pieces with a shell & his insides Lay on the grass alongside him.[12] He also belonged to my old Co. B, 48th Pa. Vols. Lieut. Wood of Co. B [was] stunned by [a] shell. Captain Gilmour, Co. H, [was] slightly wounded with [a] shell. Ebey [Alba C.] Thompson of Co. H, 48th Pa. Vols. [was] shot with [a] Minie Ball in the mouth.[13] [The] Killed, Missing & wounded up to tonight in our reigment [amounts to] 60 men.[14] Our reigment fell back to receive ammunition in the same street [on which] we war quartered in [on] the night of the 12th & tonight to our left, we hear a heavy engagement, [which is] supposed to be Franklin's Corps. Thear was a solid shot of Cannon Ball [which] went right through a house & right in range of us & we [were] dusted. We heard that Captain William Wren [B Co.] of the 129th Regt. Pa. Vol. was wounded in the foot by a shell. During the engagement at the infantry Line, we war all Lying down & the men [were] firing—Lying—& Ebey Thompson was shot & [while] being Carried to the rear, it was necessary to make room to pass the wounded & Thompson was brought through whear I was Lying & I punched the man that was Laying alongside of me, but he would not move & I got very Cross & pressed him over & after Thompson got through I turned around & said, "You're a great fellow! Why did you not move when you saw the wounded being brought Back?" & he lay Quiet & made no reply & when we examined him, he was dead as neat. He had bin shot & died instantly & we did not know it. Before going into Battle, our reigment was in line in a street & had halted for orders & while halted, thear was 6 or 7 of us sitting on a poarch [porch] on the steps. I sat next [nearest] to the enemy & while sitting thear, thear was a musket ball [which] passed my knees & shot the man next to me on my left, right in the Knee Joint & [I] neaver heard a man hallow [halloo] so in my life. He Cried, "O, I am shot! O, I am shot!" & they [the men] hooted at him & said, "How Could you get shot & [with] Major Wren sitting on your right & next to the enemy?" but we Cut his pants leg open & when it was examined, his Knee was as Black as a Coal. He was then sent off in an ambulance. I don't think his Knees on the poarch steps extended more than 6 inches farther out than mine. It made me feal a little Quear [queer] to find I had escaped so narrowly.

December 14th, 1862
In Fredricksburg, Va.

We war aroused this morning by the shelling of the enemy. It Continued but a short time [with] our guns replying. Thear was Ceveral Vollies of musketry fired by the pickets. Thear was very little firing, today being Sunday. We Camped in Captain Wells' house last night. I was walking arounds last night & I Came to a cellar whear thear was a wood fire & a lot of men & I opened the door & looked in & Capt. Winlack [E Co.] said, "Who's that?" & they said, "Major Wren." "Come in! Come in, Major! [The] men were

Just got a Copy of Robert Burns' poems and were Just reading 'The Louse on the Woman's Bonnet—the Crawlin'
Thing':

To a
Louse

I

On seeing one on a Lady's Bonnet at Church
Ha! whare ye gaun, ye crowlin ferlie!
Your impudence protects you fairly:
I canna say but ye strunt rarely.
Owre gauze and lace;
Tho' faith, I feat ye dine but sparely
On sic a place.

VIII

O wad some Pow'r the giftie gie us
To see ourselves as others see us!
It wad frae monie a blunder free us
And foolish notion;
What airs in dress an' gait wad lea'e us,
And e'en Devotion!"

I listened a while & it was amusing to see what interest the
Captain & party took in it. I left & passed along to our
Quarters. Today thear was a very amusing thing [which]
took place with Dye Davis & John Howells & Bill Hill (all
of Co. B), who was Killed with the falling of the Chimney
the day of the 12th. When we Crossed into the town of Fredricksburg, the men Captured many things & theas three,
Davis, Howells & Hill got into a house [and a] Carpenter's
store room & Dye Davis said, "We be got him now, lads. Fill
your haversacks." And the Haversacks was filled. Dye Davis
[said], "Now, lads, lets go down to the fire & we will have
some Johnny Cakes." And when they reached the fire, Dye
said, "John Howells, do we get some wood & make a fire?"
& "Bill Hill, do we get some water & I will make some
Johnny cake" & the work went on & Dye [made] a Cake on

the old plate & he turned it up to see if it was done, but [it] was not browned yet & Jack said, "Turn 'em over any'ow." & Dye turned [it] over & said, "Jack he is hard any'ow" & they got the other side hard & Dye wanted to get it browned but Bill Hill got impatient & said, "Damn, 'em, Dye, less [let's] have him!" & the Cake was handed to Bill & the Cook put another on the pan & while Dye was working at the second one, Bill Hill could not get his Knife to split the first one & Jack Howells says, "Bill, get a stone & Break 'em." & they got a stone & Broke it & tried to bite it, but it was no go & Jack examined it Carefully & exclaimed, "Damn 'em, Dye, 'e is plaster [of] Paris!" & the Cook stopped instantly & he examined & exclaimed, "Well, Jack, I did think he was Damn heavy flour in my haversack." & sure enough, it was white plaster [of] Paris.

December 15th, 1862
In Fredricksburg, Va.

[I] got up this morning. Everything [was] Very Quiet. At 8 o'clock A.M. we Commenced to move our wounded over the river to the railroad & we found out by the ambulance Corps that John Williams of Compny B, 48th Regt. Pa. Vols. died in the hospital. He was shot in the breast & the Ball Came out in [his] Back. We received orders to form line & all the Battries took theair respective places in theair Brigades. We expected to have a very heavy Battle today. We remained in line until dusk. [It was] in the evening when we received orders that our Division was to hold the town in the Center & Gen. [Erastus B.] Tyler's Division [was to hold] on the left & another Division [was to hold] on the right until our army would evacuate the town.[15] The army Crossed the pontoons in good [order]. The Night of the evacuation our reigment went up to our picket line & found another line of pickets in thear rear & [they] dug rifle pits & Drilled holes in the buildings to let the infantry fire through [them] & [still] be protected & [they used] the rifle pit for shelter & the main Body of our Brigade formed line of Battle in theair rear near the houses, throwing up earthworks sufficient to shelter the whole Brigaid line. Being 3 lines Deep off the picket Line & in [the] rear of our Brigade was Gen. Ferrero with his Brigade, in reserve to support us in Case of an attack. The rifle pits we got finished about one o'clock in the morning of the 16th. In about ½ an hour afterwards, we received orders to fall Back & Cross the pontoons as quick as possible & as Quiet as possible, which was done & the whole plan was carried out Splendid. Our whole army Crossed over, unknown to the enemy. The 129th Regt. under Col. Frick, Left in thear Quarters in Fredricksburg all [of] theair Knapsacks, Blankets & Shelter tents, which is not looked upon as being very expert. They Crossed the pontoons at 2 o'clock in the morning of the 16th & the pontoons was not withdrawn until ½ past 8 o'clock in the morning of the 16th.

December 16th, 1862
Frunt of Fredricksburg, Va.

After our reigment went into our old Camp, I went back to the Lacey House in frunt of Fredricksburg fealing anxious to see the movement of the enemy taking possession of the town & I viewed it at Daylight of the morning of the 16th. They did not venture down until between 8 & 9 o'clock A.M., when I saw the soldiers Comming down the ravine, Crawling on thear hands and feet, taking the ravine for shelter in order not to be seen. At Last they sent a flag of truce to our army & when that flag of truce returned, theair pickets Came down & took possession. They have about 2 Divisions Quartered in the town. Our pontoons was withdrawn about 9 o'clock this morning & it was a very fine sight to [see] them. I was anxious to see the movement of the engineer Corps in withdrawing the Pontoons. The movements was as follows: The Pontoons that floated remained Connected while those on the enemy's side war loosened and hauled into the floating stream and the Balance made a Grand Left wheel & they all Came to our Shoare & was immediately hauled ashore. After the pontoons was withdrawn Quite a number of our soldiers

Came too late to Cross on the pontoon Bridge & the poor fellows looked very pitiful indeed, but the pontoons was rowed over for them & they all got across & we did not Lose a man by being taken prisoners. Our whole army was a little downhearted not winning the Battle, but [was] all ready to try again.

December 17th
Opposite Fredricksburg, Va.

All Quiet along the Line of our army. We sent a flag of truce over to bury our dead that was not yet Buried & they found that the enemy had stripped our men of all theair Clothing. Stripped naked by the enemy. Our men buried 4 hundred & thear is about 250 to be buried opposite our Brigade. The enemy stated to our men that they estimated our loss to be 10 thousand & estimated theair Loss [at] 2 thousand. We did not expect the rebel side to be so large. We really find our loss to be over 6 thousand. The enemy acknowledges the Loss of 2 of theair Generals. [Thomas R.] Cobb of Georgia, nephew of Senator Cobb from Georgia, [is one of them].[16] We had inspection this morning by Gen. Nagle. Our Reigment Numbered 225 men for service. Things in Camp look Chearfull, although we did evacuate the town. We are getting things trimmed up for another trial. [We] had dress peraid this evening. I superintended the Cleaning up of Camp this afternoon with the police by request of the Col. A number of Bull Run prisoners returned today from Camp Peroal [parole] as follows: Charles Evans [Hospital Steward], Samuel Stouch, Sergeant Philip Hughes [both] of my old Compny B & many others.[17]

December 18th, 1862
Opposite Fredricksburg, Va.

All Quiet along the Lines this morning. We received orders to prepare for inspection by Gen. Nagle. Our Regt. Numbers 223 men in line. The inspection was very good in regard to the Condition of the arms. The Clothing is very poor, perticulerly the Pants.

This Book ends with the notes of the 18th of December 1862. [James Wren's final notation.]

Postscript

James Wren mustered into B Company of the 48th Pennsylvania Volunteers on September 19, 1861, for 3 years, as Captain; on September 20, 1862, he was promoted to Major; he resigned, May 20, 1863.[1]

In the Wren Papers at USAMHI our research team found a copy of his letter of resignation. It is reprinted here in its entirety.[2]

> *"Camp 48th Regt. Penn. Vols.*
> *Near Lexington Kentucky*
> *May 18th, 1863*

To Lewis Richmond, Asst. Adj. Genl.

I Major James Wren 48th Regiment Penn Vols do respectfully tender my resignation as Major of said Regiment for the following reasons herein mentioned.

I am extensively interested in the Machine business, and having a partners in it and he having had charge to carry on the business in my absence, he is now unwilling to carry on the business any longer for me, and a duty rests upon me personally on business, having laid all business aside at the breaking out of the present war, I responded to the first call of the President, and reached the Capitol for its defense on the evening of the 18th of April 1862, with my Company, and had the pleasure of being the first to enter for its defense.

My Regiment having been in active field service the last year, and has lost heavily in the different engage-

ments in which it has participated and is now reporting for duty 336 Enlisted men, twenty seven (27) line officers Col. and Lt. Col. all present for duty, it leaves but a small Command as a Regiment, and I think my services can be dispensed with, and be of no injury to the service.

> *I am Sir. Very Respectfully*
> *Your Obedt. Servt.*
> *James Wren*
> *Major 48th R"*

About the Author

According to the privately printed family history (1907), James Wren was born in 1825. In April 1861, at the age of 36, he enrolled as a captain of the Washington Artillerists. This company and four other companies left Harrisburg, Pennsylvania, for Washington, D.C., as part of the nation's response to President Abraham Lincoln's initial call for 75,000 volunteers. On April 18, 1861, the battalion (5 companies) left Harrisburg, by train, at 6:00 A.M. Twelve hours later, they detrained in the Capital. Being the first organized volunteer troops to appear upon the streets of Washington, they immediately dubbed themselves "The First Defenders".

On June 3, 1861, a large portion of those five companies mustered in as the 25th Pennsylvania Volunteers, a three month regiment. James Wren, who had voluntarily resigned his captaincy in the Washington Artillerists, enrolled as the captain of B Company of the new regiment. When the 25th Pennsylvania mustered out in September, 1861, James Wren and nine of his enlisted men signed up with the 48th Pennsylvania Volunteers for a three year commitment. Wren became the captain of B Company of this regiment. The rest of his term of service is chronicled in this diary.

Following his resignation in 1863, James Wren returned to Pottsville, Pennsylvania, to assume the presidency of a company he had started before the war. His postwar history is, unfortunately, more cryptic than his priceless diary. He married twice after he left the army, and he fathered children by both wives. His first wife, Catherine Mortimer, died at the age of 34 and is buried in Pottsville. His second wife, Clara Johns, apparently moved away with him to Boyertown, Pennsylvania. (From the diary, which contains no reference to any family except his brothers, William and Thomas, one can conclude that the captain had not yet married.)

In the 1870's Wren and other survivors of the 25th Pennsylvania Volunteers compiled a regimental history of the three month regiment. Wren also rewrote his diary in a series of addresses to the veterans of the 48th Pennsylvania as well. These papers, which are at the U.S. Army War College, Carlisle Barracks (PA), are as colorful as his diary and go into more detail concerning the earliest operations of the regiment before moving to New Bern, North Carolina. From this point, James Wren's story becomes more obscure.

His family's history recorded him as living in Boyertown, Pennsylvania, in 1907, which would have made him 82 years old.

Despite the dearth of personal information about this unique man, his diary reveals more than any biography could. The captain held no pronounced prejudices against any man, Rebel, freedman, or enlisted man. His reference to blacks as "darkeys" or "niggers", when considered in the context with which he used them, reflected his local vernacular rather than prejudice.

He meticulously captured dialects he heard spoken and his own unique accent with the skill of a trained linguist. Dye Davis of his company was a Scot. When Wren scratched the Corporal's retort that ". . . the Johnnycakes is no Dead," he recorded the typical Scottish negative response that one could find in the poems of Robert Burns. His poor spelling skills, ironically, preserved a portion of the American past which the formal historian would have sterilized. In his writing, one can literally hear the Pennsylvanian of the 1860's speaking as if into a tape recorder. If anything, the captain approached life the same as he did the war, honestly and with a bulldogged determination to see it through.

Appendix

A Guide to Captain Wren's Spelling

Captain James Wren had a definite problem with spelling and punctuation. Often erratic and seldom consistent he tended to spell words as he either pronounced them or thought he heard them pronounced or actually believed he thought they should be spelled. Punctuation seemed to be an inconvenience which cramped his writing style. (I believe he used, maybe, two or three periods in the entire manuscript and he never bothered with quotation marks at all.)

Below are some of the words which he most commonly mispelled. They indicate the Captain's unique accent and his phonetic ear. It is not a complete list of his spelling errors. Note that he tended to make one syllable words two syllable words. As the Captain would probably have advised, "Read theas words with causion and pay perticuler attenshun to how this hear fello writs what he sais." J.M.P.

acaisoneley—occasionally
adjitent, adigent, adigtant, adjentent, adjtent—adjutant
afect—effect
alick—alike
amagined—imagined
ameditly—immediately
ancious—anxious
annimel—animal
Anttedam, Antetam, Anttetan, anteatan, Antetiam—Antietam
Ashbay's—Ashby's

atmospier—atmosphere
attacted—attacked
axidently—accidentally
battry, battryes, battrey—battery
baucky—bucky [pronounced "baw key"]
baynet—bayonet
beaf—beef [pronounced "be aff"]
beaugel, bugal—bugle [pronounced "be you gall"]
bedstids—bedsteads
bin—been
blead—bled [pronounced "blay add"]
boath—both [pronounced "bo ath"]
braught—brought [pronounced "browt"]
brease—breeze
broak—broke [pronounced "bro ack"]
Brookland—Brooklyn
Burnsids, Burnsides—Burnside
butment—abutment
Carlina, Carlena—Carolina
chaplin, chaplen—chaplain
chatring—chattering
chears—cheers [pronounced "chee ars"]
coald—cold [pronounced "co auld"]
coart—court [pronounced "co art"]
Colanel, colnel—colonel
colerd—colored
compney—company
considrable—considerable
conterbands—contrabands
controale—control [pronounced "con tro al"]
coulered—colored [pronounced "cow lerd"]
coulers—colors [pronounced "cow lers"]
coult—could
creaping—creeping [pronounced "cree a ping"]
crick, crik—creek
devine—divine [pronounced "de vine"]
diarear, direar—diarrhea
difrent, diffrent—different
diret—direct
Eastren—Eastern

eather—either [pronounced "ee a ther"]
effect—affect
endfield—Enfield
enoyed—annoyed
enqury—inquiry
entrenc—entrance
entring—entering
eregular—irregular
erend—earned [pronounced "err end"]
examond—examined
excepted—accepted
extream—extreme [pronounced "ex tree am"]
feal, feals—feel [pronounced "fee al"]
feaver—fever [pronounced "fee aver"]
Febury, Febuary—February
finely—finally
foard—ford [pronounced "fo ard"]
foot lock—fetlock
forough—furrow
Fredrick—Frederick
Fredricksburg—Fredericksburg
fust—first
gardains—gardens
genrel—general
goverment—government
granmother—grandmother
harbert—harbor
hasers—hausers
hazerts—hazards
heals—heels [pronounced "he als"]
hear—here [pronounced as "he are"]
hollow—halloo
honer—honor
ificent—efficient
imbarked—embarked
infintry—infantry
instent—instant
instinteley—instantly
iver—over [pronounced with a short "i" as "iv er"]
Kator, Keator—caterer

keept—kept
kitls—kettles [pronounced "kittles"]
lafter—laughter
larkert—larbard
lenth—length
malishe—militia [pronounced "ma leash"]
markeys—marquees [pronounced "marr keys"]
Meryland, Myrland—Maryland [pronounced "Murry land"]
Middleton—Middletown
mustring—mustering
neather—neither [pronounced "knee a ther"]
neaver—never [pronounced "knee ver"]
Newhamshier, newhamshir, Newhanshir, Newhanshier—New
  Hampshire
ocationaley—occasionally
oppertunity—opportunity
oppning—opening
orgenising—organizing [pronounced "or gen eye sing"]
perad, peraid—parade [pronounced "per aid"]
percisly—precisely
perfit, perfict—perfect
perole—parole
perticipate—participate
perticular, perticuler—particular
perticuly—particularly
pertisipent—participant
photegrafs—photographs [pronounced "pho tee graphs"]
pionear—pioneer [pronounced "pie o knee ar"]
posision—position
posponed—postponed
pottatas—potatoes
Pottomik, Potomik, Pottomich—Potomac
poured—poured [pronounced "pow erd"]
practising—practicing
proceded—preceded
principly—principally
proceedid—proceeded
quaver—quiver
rair—rear [pronounced "rare"]
rait—right

Rapahanick—Rappahannock
rashons, rashions, rasions—rations [pronounced "rash ons"]
read—red [pronounced "re ad"]
regmental, regamental—regimental
reguler—regular
Reigment, rigment, rigmet—regiment
Rhoad—Rhode [pronounced "row ad"]
roale—roll [pronounced "row al"]
sanatary—sanitary
scabert—scabbard
sevrel—several
shoare—sure
shoos, shooes—shoes [pronounced with a soft "s"]
showr—shower [pronounced "shaur"]
sid—said
sinu—sinew
snigered—snickered
Sniger's—Snicker's
starbert—starboard
steared—steered
suckseed—succeed
sucksessful[ly]—successful
sucksesser—successor
sufert—suffered
sufring—suffering
surgon—surgeon
tack-tick—tactic
teath—teeth [pronounced "tee ath"]
thar—there
thear, theare, theair—their [pronounced as "the are"]
theas—these [pronounced "thee as"]
then—than
thoes—those [pronounced "though es"]
Tigar—tiger yell
tolarable—tolerable
traitorisom—traitorism
tricker—trigger
war, ware—were
weaks—weeks [pronounced "wee aks"]
Wensday—Wednesday

whear—where [pronounced "whee are"]
widning—widening
Wilksberey—Wilkes Barre
Windfield—Winfield
wood—would

Footnotes

Chapter 1
The North Carolina Expedition

[1]Samuel P. Bates, "Forty-Eighth Regiment," *History of Pennsylvania Volunteers*, Vol. I. B. Singerly, State Printers, Harrisburg, PA. 1869, p. 1861–1862.

The 48th Pennsylvania arrived at Hatteras Island, North Carolina on November 12, 1861 and went into temporary quarters at Fort Clark. Shortly after its arrival, the regiment, B Company excepted, moved five miles from the inlet to comfortable wooden barracks which they named Camp Winfield. B Company remained at Fort Clark until February 20, 1862, the date that the diary begins.

[2]*Ibid.*, p. 1208.

Wood, John L., B Co., PA. Mustered in, September 19, 1861, for 3 years, as 2nd Lieutenant; promoted to 1st Lieutenant, September 20, 1862; resigned, December 30, 1862.

Throughout the diary, Captain Wren always referred to his faithful lieutenant as "Woods". Captain Oliver C. Bosbyshell (G Co.) in his book, *The 48th in the War,* also refers to the lieutenant as "Woods".

[3]Rhode Island Adjutant General's Office. *Official Roster of Rhode Island Officers and Soldiers Who Served in the United States Army and Navy, From, 1861 to 1866,* by order of the General Assembly, January Session, 1866, p. 765.

Pope, Charles H., Battery F. 1st Regiment Rhode Island Light Artillery. Mustered in October 17, 1861; resigned October 6, 1862.

[4]Ezra J. Warner, *Generals in Blue*, Louisiana State University Press, p. 563–564.

Williams, Thomas, Born: January 10, 1815, Albany, NY; private during the Black Hawk War; 1833 entered West Point; graduated from West Point 1837 as artillery subaltern; 1837–1844 served in Seminole war, garrison duty and as an instructor at West Point; 1844–1850 aide-de-camp to General Winfield Scott and was brevetted to captain and later major for gallantry during the Mexican War; 1850–1860 more garrison duty and further action against the Seminoles and also against Western tribes; 1861 Artillery School for Practice at Fortress Monroe; 1861-May 14; major in the 5th Artillery; September 28; brigadier general of volunteers; September-October; acting inspector general of the Department of Virginia; C.O. 5th Artillery in Philadelphia; October; participated in Burnside's Hatteras Expedition, October 1861-March 1862; C.O. of Fort Hatteras, NC; March 1862-August 1862; Served in New Orleans and Baton Rouge, LA; 1862-August 5; Shot and killed by a musket ball in the chest during an attack by Confederates upon Baton Rouge.

Bates, Vol. 1, p. 1203.

Nagle, James, Staff, 48th PA. Mustered in, October 1, 1861 as Colonel of 48th PA; promoted to Brigadier General, September 10, 1862; resigned May 9, 1863.

[5]*Ibid.*, p. 1208.

Bast, Ulysses A., B Co., 48th PA. Mustered in, September 19, 1861, for 3 years, as 1st Lieutenant; promoted to Captain, September 20, 1862; mustered out September 30, 1864—expiration of term.

[6]Connecticut, Adjutant General's Office. *Record of Service of Connecticut Men in the Army and Navy of the United States During the War of the Rebellion.* Press of the Case, Lockwood, and Brainard Company, Hartford, CT. 1889, P. 434.

Southmayd, George M., A Co., 11th CT, Enlisted, September 5, 1861 as Captain; mustered in, November 27, 1861; resigned, July 18, 1862.

Bailey Samuel G., A Co., 11th CT, Enlisted September 5, 1861 as 1st Lieutenant; mustered in, November 27, 1861; Promoted to Captain of B Co., March 18, 1862.

[7]Bates, Vol. 1, p. 1204.

Jackson, Abiel H., A Co., 48th PA. Mustered in, for 3 years, September 17, 1861 as 1st Lieutenant; resigned September 29, 1862.

[8]*Ibid.*, p. 1203, 1204 and 1211.

Loeser, Charles, G Co., 48th PA. Mustered in, October 1, 1861, for 3 years, as Private; promoted to Sergeant Major by February 25, 1862; promoted September 26, 1862 to 2nd Lieutenant, C Company; promoted January 1, 1864 to 1st Lieutenant; promoted June 25, 1864 to Adjutant; mustered out, October 1, 1864—expiration of term.

[9]*Ibid.*, p. 1232.

Brannan, Isaac F., K Co., 48th PA. Mustered in, October 1, 1861, for 3 years, as 1st Lieutenant; promoted to Captain, August 30, 1862; mustered out, October 6, 1864—expiration of term.

[10]*Ibid.*, p. 1226.

Miller, Charles H., H Co., 48th PA. Mustered in, January 16, 1862, for 3 years, as 2nd Lieutenant; resigned, date unknown.

[11]*Ibid.*, p. 1211, and 1203.

Pleasants, Henry, C Co., 48th PA. Mustered in, September 11, 1861, for 3 years, as Captain; promoted to Lieutenant Colonel, September 20, 1862; mustered out, December 18, 1864—expiration of term; promoted to brevet Brigadier General, March 13, 1865.

Captain Ballance, apparently, was a resident of Hatteras. Wren mentions him later on in his diary.

[12]*Ibid.*, p. 1203 and 1214.

Reber, Charles T., Surgeon, 48th PA. Mustered in, October 1, 1861, for 3 years, as Assistant Surgeon; promoted to Surgeon, February 14, 1862; resigned February 23, 1863.

Nagle, Daniel, D Co., 48th PA. Enrolled, September 23, 1861, for 3 years, as Captain; promoted November 30, 1861 to Major; resigned, July 26, 1862.

[13]*Ibid.*, p. 1223 and 1203.

Bosbyshell, Oliver C., G Co., 48th PA. Mustered in, for 3 years, as 2nd Lieutenant; promoted May 5, 1862 to 1st Lieutenant; promoted June 2, 1862 to Captain; promoted July 23, 1864 to Major; Mustered out, October 1, 1864—expiration of term.

[14]*Ibid.*, p. 1220.

James, Henry, F Co., 48th PA. Mustered in, October 1, 1861, for 3 years, as 1st Lieutenant; discharged on a surgeon's certificate, June 26, 1864.

[15]*Ibid.*, p. 1232.

Douty, Jacob, K Co., 48th PA. Mustered in, October 1, 1861, for 3 years, as 2nd Lieutenant; promoted August 29, 1862 to 1st Lieutenant; Mustered out, September 30, 1864—expiration of term.

[16]Oliver C. Bosbyshell. *The 48th in the War*, Avil Printing Co., Philadelphia, p. 38–51.

Captain Bosbyshell's "Newbern" Chapter contains many excellent recollections of the campaign which follows in Wren's diary.

[17]Bates, Vol. 1. p. 1210.

Root, Daniel, B Co., 48th PA. Mustered in, September 19, 1861, for three years, as a private; captured, date not stated; died September 14, 1862 in Andersonville Prison. Georgia—grave number 8,742.

[18]Bosbyshell, p. 38–39.

Gallaway died as a result of his wounds. Captain Bosbyshell described the drunkeness as "orgies." Whiskey dealers had used the 12th to hustle whiskey in their boats to the beached regiment.

[19]William H. Powell and Edward Shippen. *Officers of the Army and Navy*. L. R. Hamersly and Co., Philadelphia, PA, 1892, p. 147.

Flagler, Daniel W., Graduated from West Point, June 28, 1861 as a brevet 2nd Lieutenant or ordnance; promoted to 1st Lieutenant, August 3, 1861; August-December 1861, ordnance officer at Allegheny Arsenal, Fort Pitt Foundry; December 1861-August 1862, chief of ordnance to Burnside's North Carolina Expedition; September-October 1862, aide-de-camp and assistant ordnance officer in the IX Corps; October 1862-May 1865, staff duty in ordnance in New York, Washington, DC, and, at the end of the war, Richmond, VA.

[20]Francis B. Heitman, *Historical Register and Dictionary of the United States Army,* Vol. I, U.S. Government Printing Office, Washington, DC, 1903. (Reprint, University of Illinois, 1965), p. 728.

Morris, Lewis Owen, 2nd Lieutenant, 1st U.S. Artillery, March 8, 1847; 1st Lieutenant, December 23, 1847; Captain, April 21, 1861; enrolled as Colonel, 7th NY Artillery, August 14, 1862; killed, June 4, 1864 at Cold Harbor, VA.

[21]Our team was not able to identify Captain Colyer.

[22]Weymouth T. Jordon, Jr., *North Carolina Troops 1861–1865,* Vol. IX, Division of Archives and History, Raleigh. NC, p. 118.

Avery, Clark Moulton, Captain, G Co., 1st NC for 6 months in 1861; appointed Lieutenant Colonel, 33rd NC, on or about November 14, 1861; promoted to Colonel, January 17, 1862; captured at New Berne, March 14, 1862; confined at Fort Columbus, NY; transferred to Johnson's Island, Ohio, June 1862; sent to Vicksburg, MS. September 1862; exchanged at Aiken's Landing, James River, VA, November 10, 1862; wounded at Chancellorsville, VA, between May 1–9, 1863; wounded at the Wilderness, VA, between May 5–6, 1864; died of his wound, Orange Court House, VA, June 18, 1864.

[23]Bates, Vol. 1, p. 1214.

Kleckner, Charles, D Co., 48th PA. Mustered in, September 23, 1861, for 3 years, as 2nd Lieutenant; promoted January 1, 1862 to 1st Lieutenant; promoted to Colonel of the 172nd PA, December 1, 1862.

[24]*Ibid.,* p. 1203.

Sigfried, Joshua K., Staff, 48th PA. Mustered in, October 1, 1861, for 3 years, as Major; promoted November 30, 1861 to Lieutenant Colonel; promoted September 20, 1862 to Colonel; promoted to Brevet Brigadier General, August 1, 1864; mustered out, October 11, 1864—expiration of term.

[25]*Record of Service of Connecticut Men*, p. 455.

Rice, Randall, H., G Co., 11th CT, Enlisted, September 20, 1861; mustered in November 12, 1861 as 1st Sergeant; promoted March 28, 1862 to 2nd Lieutenant; promoted October 27, 1862 to 1st Lieutenant, I Co.; promoted January 1, 1863 to Captain, I Co.; wounded, May 4; 1863 at Providence Church Road, VA; wounded June 18, 1864 at Petersburg, VA; discharged with a disability October 31, 1864; mustered out November 25, 1864 as Major.

[26]Bates, Vol. 1, p. 1214.

Potts, William W., D Co., 48th PA, Mustered in, September 23, 1861, for 3 years, as 1st Lieutenant; promoted November 30, 1861; discharged, January 3, 1863.

[27]Warner, *Generals in Blue*, p. 57–58.

Burnside, Ambrose Everett, Born May 23, 1824, Liberty, Indiana; graduated from West Point in 1847 as a brevet 2nd Lieutenant in the 2nd U.S. Artillery; served in garrison duty in Mexico City and in 1849 was wounded in a skirmish with the Apaches; resigned in 1853 to enter weapons manufacture business; the venture failed; between then and 1861 he served in Congress, worked with the Illinois Central Railroad, and was appointed a major general in the state militia; 1861, he formed the 1st Rhode Island Infantry; brigade commander at the First Manassas; August 6, 1861 appointed brigadier general of volunteers; commander of the North Carolina Expedition; March 18, 1862 promoted to major general; September 1862, wing commander in charge of the I and the IX Corps; November 10, 1862, commanded to take over the Army of the Potomac; March 1863, assigned commander of the Department of the Ohio; spring 1864, appointed commander of the IX Corps; resigned April 15, 1865 following the Battle of the Crater, Petersburg, VA, July, 1864; postwar, elected three times to governorship of Rhode Island; died September 13, 1881.

[28]Bates, Vol. I, p. 1204.
Kauffman, Daniel B., A Co., 48th PA, Mustered in, September 17, 1861, for 3 years, as Captain; dismissed August 1, 1864.

[29]Koons and Isaac Lippman apparently were civilian sutlers with the 48th Pennsylvania. They do not appear on the roster.

[30]Bates, Vol. I, p. 1204 and 1226.
Brown, Alexander S., H Co., 48th PA, Mustered in, September 19, 1861, for 3 years, as Sergeant; promoted October 1, 1861 to Regimental Quartermaster Sergeant; promoted October 11, 1861 to 2nd Lieutenant; promoted August 28, 1863 to 1st Lieutenant; mustered out, September 30, 1864—expiration of term. (He is also listed as Alex S. Bowen.)

[31]Warner, *Generals in Blue*, p. 394–395.
Reno, Jesse Lee, Born June 20, 1823, Wheeling, VA; graduated from West Point in 1846; breveted to 1st Lieutenant and Captain for gallantry during Mexican War; January 1861, surrendered the Mount Vernon Arsenal (AL) to state forces; November 12, 1861, promoted to brigadier general; brigade commander with Burnside's North Carolina Expedition; April-August 1862, in command of a division in the Federal Department of North Carolina; August 20, 1862, appointed major general; Commander of the IX Corps at Second Manassas, Chantilly (both VA), and Fox's Gap, MD; died of his wounds at Fox's Gap on September 14, 1862.

[32]*Ibid.*, p. 157–158.
Foster, John Gray. Born May 27, 1823, Whitfield, NH; graduated from West Point in 1846; won two brevets during the Mexican War; participated in the bombardment of Fort Sumter, SC, April 1861; October 1862 promoted from captain in engineers to brigadier general; took part in Burnside's North Carolina Expedition; July 1862, assigned to command the Department of North Carolina; Autumn 1863 replaced Burnside as commander of the Army; December 1863 promoted to commander of the Department of Ohio; resigned in February 1864 because of injuries sustained when a horse fell on him; 1865 returned to duty as commander of the Department of the South and then the Department of Florida; March 1865 promoted to major general; died September 2, 1874.

[33]Bates, Vol. I, p. 1229.

Gressang, George H., I Co., 48th PA, Mustered in, August 23, 1861, for 3 years, as 1st Lieutenant; drowned during the sinking of the "West Point", August 12, 1862.

[34]*Official Roster of Rhode Island Officers and Soldiers*, p. 765.

Belger, James, Battery F. 1st Rhode Island Light Artillery, Mustered in, October 17, 1861 as Captain; wounded severely in leg, April 9, 1863 near New Bern. NC; missing, May 16, 1864. Drury's Bluff. VA; prisoner of war, escaped. December, 1864; mustered out, December 30, 1864.

[35]Bates, Vol. I, p. 1232.

Filbert, H.A.M., K Co., 48th PA. Mustered in, October 1, 1861, for 3 years, as Captain; killed in action, August 29, 1862 at 2nd Bull Run.

[36]New York Adjutant General *Report*, 1896, p. 301.

Ledlie, James H., age 29. Enrolled, May 18, 1861; mustered in as Major, 19th NY, May 22, 1861, for 2 years; mustered in as Lieutenant Colonel September 28, 1861; promoted to Colonel, November 1, 1861; regimental designation changed to 3rd New York Artillery, December 11, 1861; promoted to Brigadier General, December 24, 1862.

[37]Bates, Vol. I. p. 1203.

Smith, David A., Staff, 48th PA, Commissioned as Lieutenant Colonel, August 20, 1861, but not mustered; resigned, November 1861.

[38]*Ibid.*, p. 1208.

Johnston, Joseph, B Co., 48th PA, Mustered in, September 19, 1861, for 3 years, as a musician; promoted to corporal before April 10, 1862; mustered out, September 21, 1864—expiration of term.

[39]Bosbyshell, p. 45–46.

Captain Bosbyshell said the uniform consisted of blacked shoes, white gloves, paper collars, light blue trousers, which replaced the dark blue they had been wearing, and Enfield Rifles, which replaced their Harper's Ferry muskets.

[40]Gould, Joseph, *The Story of the Forty-Eighth*, Regimental Association, 1908, p. 407.

Bates, Vol. I, p. 1209 and 1210.

Marsden, George, B Co., 48th PA, Mustered in, September 19, 1861, for 3 years, as Private; deserted, date not stated; returned, date not stated; mustered out with Company, July 17, 1865.

Conell, Thomas, B Co., 48th PA, Mustered in, September 19, 1861, for 3 years, as Private; not on muster out roll; died, December 18, 1862 of disease.

[41]Thompson, Herbert S., *First Defenders*, 1910, p. 76–83.

Bosbyshell, p. 46.

The "First Defenders", officially known as the 25th Pennsylvania

Volunteers, earned their sobriquet because they were the first Federal troops to enter Washington, DC. The regiment, which consisted of five companies, mustered in at Harrisburg, Pennsylvania at 6:00 A.M., April 18, 1861 and arrived in Washington, DC at 6:00 P.M. the same day.

Captain Wren's Washington Artillery, which was a militia unit from Pottsville, Pennsylvania, became part of B Company of the 25th Pennsylvania Volunteers. He organized this company at Fort Washington, Maryland on June 3, 1861. They mustered out on July 18, 1861 at the end of their three months' enlistment and Captain Wren turned their newly acquired Springfield Rifles over to the government on July 28, 1861.

The roster indicates that several of Wren's "Washington Artillerists" transferred to the 48th Pennsylvania.

> James Wren, age 36, Captain, B Co., 48th PA.
> Joseph A. Gilmour, age 26, Captain, H Co., 48th PA.
> Cyrus Sheetz, age 32, 1st Lieutenant, G Co., 48th PA.
> George H. Gressang, age 24, 1st Lieutenant, I Co., 48th PA.
> Thomas Johnson, age 47, Sergeant, B Co., 48th PA.
> Lewis Douglass, age 24, Private, I Co., 48th PA.
> Nelson Drake, age 27, Private, K Co., 48th PA.
> John C. Weaver, age 27, Private, B Co., 48th PA.
> David Williams, age 23, Private, E Co., 48th PA.

Captain Bosbyshell recalled that the members of the "First Defenders" met in a house near the camp and that there was much "jollification." Since April 18 also marked the creation of that entire regiment there were, obviously, more people from Wren's old company there.

Boyer, Henry, A Co., 48th PA; Mustered in, September 17, 1861 for 3 years; promoted from 2nd to 1st Lieutenant September 29, 1862; promoted to Captain, August 27, 1864; mustered out October 1, 1864, expiration of term.

[42]Warner, *Generals in Blue*, p. 150–151.

Ferrero, Edward, Born January 18, 1831, Granada, Spain; before the war, he became a dancing instructor at West Point; April 1861, Lieutenant Colonel in charge of a militia regiment; October 14, 1861, mustered in as Colonel of the 51st NY; commanded a brigade, but not promoted to general rank, after New Bern; promoted to brigadier general following Battle at Antietam, MD, September 17, 1862, but was not confirmed by the Senate; reappointed brigadier general May 6, 1863; brigade and division commander at Vicksburg, MS and Knoxville, TN, respectively; 1864 commander of newly created colored division of the IX Corps; failed miserably at the Battle of the Crater, July 30, 1864; (He was in a bombproof area behind the lines with General Ledlie—drinking); promoted nonetheless to brevet major general for "meritorious service" in that campaign; died, December 11, 1899.

[43]Bates, Vol. I, p. 1224 and 1233.

Sillyman, Edward H., G Co., 48th PA, Mustered in, October 1, 1861, for 3 years, as Corporal; promoted, date unknown, to Sergeant; mustered out with company, July 17, 1865—veteran.

Drake, Nelson, K Co., 48th PA, Mustered in, October 1, 1861, for 3 years, as Private; mustered out, September 30, 1864—expiration of term.

[44]*Ibid.*, p. 1211.

Gould, p. 410.

Sheck, Paul, B Co., 48th PA, Mustered in, September 19, 1861, for 3 years, as Private; sick in hospital October 21, 1862 in Knoxville, TN; not on muster out roll.

[45]*Ibid.*, p. 1203 and 1211.

Gowen, George W., C Co., 48th PA, Mustered in, September 11, 1861, for 3 years, as 1st Lieutenant; promoted, January 1, 1864 to Captain; promoted December 20, 1864 to Lieutenant Colonel; promoted March 1, 1865 to Colonel; killed at Petersburg, VA, April 2, 1865.

Bosbyshell, p. 46.

During the fight for Fort Macon, NC, Gowen assumed the role of acting officer in Battery C, 1st U.S. Artillery.

Warner, *Generals in Blue*, p. 359–360.

Parke, John Grubb. Born September 22, 1827, near Coatsville, PA; graduated from West Point in 1849; before the Civil War he served in the Corps of Topographical Engineers and the Corps of Engineers in survey work on the U.S.—Canada border; November 23, 1861 promoted to brigadier general with a brigade during the North Carolina Expedition; promoted to major general on August 20, 1862; during the Maryland Campaign served as Burnside's chief of staff; commanded the IX Corps at Vicksburg and Knoxville; during the Overland Campaign of 1864 again served as Burnside's chief of staff; commanded IX Corps when Burnside was relieved following the Crater debacle; temporarily commanded the Army of the Potomac during the attack on Fort Stedman, VA, on March 25, 1865; retired from the Army in 1889 as a colonel of engineers; died December 16, 1900.

[46]Bates, Vol. I, p. 1204, 1223 and 1229.

Auman, William, G Co., 48th PA, Mustered in, October 1, 1861, for 3 years, as Private; promoted to Corporal then Sergeant by April 30, 1862; promoted July 24, 1864 to 2nd Lieutenant; promoted September 12, 1864 to 1st Lieutenant; promoted March 3, 1865 to Brevet Captain; promoted June 4, 1865 to Captain; mustered out with company, July 17, 1865—veteran.

Wagner, Jacob, H Co., 48th PA, Mustered in, September 19, 1861, for 3 years, as a private; promoted October 4, 1861 to Regimental Quartermaster Sergeant; promoted December 27, 1862 to Regimental Quartermaster; promoted June 21, 1865 to Major; mustered out with regiment, July 17, 1865.

[47]*Ibid.*, p. 1208.

Johnson, Thomas, B Co., 48th PA, Mustered in, September 19, 1861, for 3 years, as Sergeant; promoted September 1, 1863 to 2nd Lieutenant; promoted July 24, 1864 to 1st Lieutenant; discharged on surgeon's certificate, August 7, 1864.

FOOTNOTES

[48]*Ibid.*, p. 1203, 1204, and 1217.

Warner, *Generals in Blue*, p. 290–292.

McClellan, George Brinton, Born on December 3, 1826 in Philadelphia, PA; graduated from West Point in 1846; brevetted to 1st lieutenant and captain during the Mexican War; between the Mexican War and the Civil War, he taught at West Point, explored the Red River, traveled abroad to study the armies in the Crimean War, designed the "McClellan Saddle;" 1857 resigned to become chief engineer on the Illinois Central RR; 1861 was president of the Ohio & Mississippi RR; became a major general of Ohio Volunteers on April 23, 1861; three weeks later, President Lincoln appointed him major general in the Regular Army; defeated the Confederates at Rich Mountain early in the war; on November 1, 1861, he became General-in-Chief of the Armies of the United States; commanded the Army of the Potomac through the Peninsular Campaign until replaced by Pope; after the 2nd Manassas, he was given command of the Army through the Antietam Campaign; November 7, 1862 he was ordered to turn the command of the Army over to Ambrose Burnside for his failure to pursue Lee after Antietam; attempted to win the Presidency of the United States as a Democrat on a "peace" ticket; resigned his commission on election day; 1878–1881 served as Governor of New Jersey; died on October 29, 1885.

Schnerr, Charles W., Staff, 48th PA, Mustered in, October 1, 1861, for 3 years, as Regimental Quartermaster Sergeant; promoted to Sergeant Major, date unknown; promoted March 16, 1864 to 2nd Lieutenant, E Company; promoted October 30, 1864 to Captain; mustered out with company, July 17, 1865—veteran.

Holman, Samuel A., Staff, 48th PA, Mustered in, October 1, 1861, for 3 years, as Chaplain; resigned, January 2, 1863.

[49]*Ibid.*, p. 1210–1211.

Gould, p. 409, 410.

Williams, John W., B Co., 48th PA, Mustered in, September 19, 1861, for 3 years, as Private; discharged May 12, 1862, New Bern, NC.

Molsen, David W., B Co., 48th PA, Mustered in, September 19, 1861, for 3 years, as Private; discharged May 12, 1862, New Bern, NC.

[50]*Ibid.*, p. 1220.

Hoskings, Joseph H., H Co., 48th PA, Mustered in, October 1, 1861, for 3 years, as Captain; mustered out, September 30, 1864—expiration of term.

[51]*Record of Service of Connecticut Men*, p. 414.

Branch, Joseph W., F Co., 10th CT, Enrolled August 29, 1861; mustered in, October 1, 1861; resigned, January 24, 1863.

[52]Bosbyshell, p. 46.

Captain Bosbyshell noted that Companies E, F, G, and K returned to the regiment and that there was much merriment and handshaking.

[53]Bates, Vol. I, p. 1223.

Pollock, Curtis C., G Co., 48th PA, Mustered in, October 1, 1861, for 3 years, as Corporal; promoted May 5, 1862 to 2nd Lieutenant; promoted June 2, 1862 to 1st Lieutenant; wounded, June 17, 1864; died of wounds, June 23, 1864.

Curtis C. Pollock Letters, Civil War Miscellaneous Collection, USAMHI.

In a series of letters to his father and his mother, Curtis Pollock complained bitterly about his treatment by Colonel Joshua Sigfried of the 48th Pennsylvania.

May 17, 1862 to father.

"*My commission arrived this morning but Lt. Col. Seigfried [sic] who is now in command of the regiment will not recognize it. If you can see the Governor at once I think it will be all right as it is all spite on the Lt. Col. side as he is angry that he knew nothing about it . . .*"

May 28, 1862 to father.

"*I was over to see the Lt. Col. this morning to see why he would not recognize me and he says that he recommended Charlie Leoser [Sergeant Major Charles Leoser] and he does not think that the Governor has any right to appoint anybody but him especially if they are not recommended by some person in higher rank. He also thinks that I have no right to go above all the sergeants in the company, so he has written to the Governor to ask him what he means, so I will soon find out and I hope it will turn out all right . . . I am going down to see Col. Nagle this morning and see what he says about it. Lt. Col. Seigfried says he has nothing against me but, in the Governor's appointing he goes against his own orders . . .*"

May 30, 1862 to father.

"*. . . The Capt. [This is a mental slip. Pollock, apparently, means Colonel Nagle] was very angry when he found out that Seigfried would not give it to me and he went and told him to give it to me as he and Bosbyshell were both satisfied but he [Sigfried] would not give it to me as he, nor did he, even notify me of his having received it [the commission] and when Bosbyshell (who is acting Adjutant) asked him if he should put my name in the order to be read out at Dress Parade, he said "he would be court martialed first . . .*"

June 6, 1862 to mother.

"*. . . What do you think of Seigfried's behavior? I only hope the Governor will give him what he deserves and court martial him." He is very unpopular and all the men I have spoken to about myself say I must not let a stone unturned until I get righted again . . .*"

The Lieutenant finally received his commission on June 22, 1864. During this entire time, he made no mention of Captain Wren and their conversation at all.

[54]Bates, Vol. 1, p. 1204.

Brown, Frederick J., Staff, 48th PA, Mustered in, August 24, 1861, for 3 years, as Musician; discharged by General Order, August 24, 1862.

Maize, William A., Staff, 48th PA, Mustered in, August 24, 1861, for 3 years, as Musician; discharged by General Order, August 18, 1862.

[55]*Ibid.*, p. 1210.

Gould, p. 409.

Knittle, Frederick, B Co., 48th PA, Mustered in, September 19, 1861, for 3 years, as Private; Wounded at Antietam, MD, September 17, 1862; killed, May 12, 1864, Spotsylvania Court House, VA; buried on the battlefield.

[56]*Ibid.*, p. 1226, 1203, and 1229.

Gilmour, Joseph A., H Co., 48th PA, Mustered in, September 19, 1861, for 3 years, as Captain; promoted July 28, 1863 to Major; wounded May 31, 1864; died of wounds June 9, 1864.

Porter, John R., I Co., 48th PA, Mustered in, August 23, 1861, for 3 years, as Captain; discharged December 30, 1862.

[57]*Ibid.*, p. 1222.

Phillips, John, F Co., 48th PA, Mustered in, October 1, 1861, for 3 years, as Private; mustered out, September 30, 1864—expiration of term.

Corporal Weaver does not appear on the rolls in Bates' account. Our research team has not been able to locate him as of this time.

[58]*Ibid.*, p. 1211.

Fitzsimmons, Thomas J., C Co., 48th PA, Mustered in, September 11, 1861, for 3 years, as 2nd Lieutenant; promoted September 28, 1862 to 1st Lieutenant; resigned November 22, 1862.

[59]Alfred S. Roe, *Twenty-Fourth Regiment Massachusetts Volunteers, 1861–1866, "New England Guard Regiment"*, 1907, p. 450.

Stevenson, Thomas G., age 25, Staff, 24th MA, Enrolled, August 31, 1861 as Colonel; promoted December 26, 1862 to Brigadier General; killed May 10, 1864 at Spotsylvania Court House, VA, while commanding the 1st Division of the IX Corps.

[60]To date, our team has not been able to identify Vice Captain Messinger.

[61]Bates, Vol. I, p. 1220.

Williams, John L., F Co., 48th PA, Mustered in, October 1, 1861, for 3 years, as 2nd Lieutenant; promoted July 13, 1864 to 1st Lieutenant; promoted October 30, 1864 to Captain; mustered out with Company, July 17, 1865.

[62]Massachusetts' Adjutant General, *Massachusetts Soldiers, Sailors, and Marines in the Civil War*, Vol. II, Norwood Press, Norwood, MA, 1931, p. 596.

Hall, Theron E., age 39, Adjutant, 21st MA, Commissioned and mustered September 18, 1861 as Adjutant; discharged July 28, 1862.

[63]Bates, Vol. I, p. 1204 and 1223.

Hardell, William, H., G Co., 48th PA, Mustered in, October 1, 1861, for 3 years, as Corporal; promoted October 1, 1861 to Hospital Steward; promoted September 15, 1864 to 2nd Lieutenant, G Company; promoted June 4, 1865 to 1st Lieutenant; mustered out with Company, July 17, 1865—veteran.

[64]*Ibid.*, p. 1208.
Hume, William H., B Co., 48th PA, Mustered in, September 19, 1861, for 3 years, as 1st Sergeant; promoted September 20, 1862 to 2nd Lieutenant; promoted September 1, 1863 to 1st Lieutenant; wounded in action, May 31, 1864; died of wounds, June 30, 1864.

[65]*Ibid.*, p. 1204 and 1214.
Owens, Henry P., D Co., 48th PA, Mustered in, September 23, 1861, for 3 years, as 1st Sergeant; promoted February 5, 1862 to 2nd Lieutenant; resigned November 27, 1862.
Haas, Edward L., Staff, 48th PA, Mustered in, August 24, 1861, for 3 years, as Musician; discharged by General Order, August 18, 1862.

Chapter 2
Virginia

[1]Bates, Vol. I, p. 1217.
Shaeffer, Mattis, D Co., 48th PA, Mustered in, September 23, 1861, for 3 years, as Private; not on muster out rolls.

[2]*Ibid.*, p. 1208–1211.
Gould, p. 406, 410.
Campbell, Robert, B Co., 48th PA, Mustered in, September 19, 1861, for 3 years, as Private; promoted May 23, 1865 to 1st Sergeant; mustered out with Company, July 17, 1865—veteran.
Kirby, Joseph, B Co., 48th PA, Mustered in, September 19, 1861, for 3 years, as Corporal; sick in hospital, September 23, 1862; not on muster out roll.
Stanley, Samuel, B Co., 48th PA, Mustered in, September 19, 1861, for 3 years, as private; missing in action, August 29, 1862, Bull Run, VA; not on muster out rolls.

[3]*Ibid.*, p. 1118.
Matthews, Joseph A., Staff, 46th PA, Mustered in, September 27, 1861, for 3 years as Captain, A Company; promoted September 27, 1861 to Major.

[4]Werner, *Generals in Blue*, p. 297–299.
McDowell, Irvin, Born October 15, 1818, Columbus, Ohio; graduated from West Point in 1838; 1841–1861 taught tactics at West Point, served as aide-de-camp to General Wool during Mexican War, and, until the Civil War served as adjutant general of the army; May 14, 1861, through the influence of Secretary of the Treasury, Salmon P. Chase, he was appointed a brigadier general in the Regulars; March, 1862 promoted to major general of volunteers and made a corps commander in the Army of the Potomac; during the Second Manassas, he commanded the III Corps; following a court of inquiry about his behavior during that campaign, he was "exonerated" and after a two year absence was given the command

of the Department of the Pacific on July 1, 1864; died May 4, 1885.

Banks, Nathaniel Prentiss. Born January 30, 1816, Waltham, MA. Worked as a boy in his father's cotton mill; had little formal education; admitted to the bar at age 23; after seven attempts was elected to the Massachusetts legislature; served as speaker of the Massachusetts house; presided over the Constitutional Convention of 1853; elected to the House of Representatives in 1853; in 1856 became the Speaker of the House; 1858 elected as Governor of Massachusetts; in January, 1861 became a major general of volunteers by Presidential appointment when Banks asked for the position; served well as a good financial contributor, morale raiser, and propagandist but failed miserably as an officer; in 1862 he lost the Shenandoah campaign to T. J. Jackson and lost to him again that August at Cedar Mountain; he also lost at Port Hudson during the Vicksburg campaign and again at the Red River in 1864; General E. R. S. Canby replaced him and Banks mustered out of the service in 1865, with a commendation from the U.S. Congress; that August he won another seat in Congress in which he served six more terms—five as a Republican and one as a Democrat; he also served as the U.S. marshal for the state of Massachusetts; he retired from the House of Representatives in 1894 and died at his home in Waltham on September 1 of that year.

Ezra J. Warner, *Generals in Gray*, Louisiana State University Press, Baton Rouge, LA, p. 151–152.

Jackson, Thomas Jonathan "Stonewall", Born January 21, 1824, Clarksburg, VA; graduated from West Point in 1846; won brevets to captain and major during the Mexican War; resigned in 1852 to become an instructor at the Virginia Military Institute; April, 1861, colonel of a Virginia militia unit in command of Harper's Ferry; June 17, 1861 promoted to brigadier general; October 7, 1861 promoted to major general; during the Valley Campaign of 1862, he distinguished himself by rapid marches and hard fighting; September 15, 1862 captured Harper's Ferry; October 10, 1862 promoted to lieutenant general; December 1862 commanded the right wing of the Army of Northern Virginia at Fredericksburg; wounded by his own men by accident on the night of May 2, 1863; died of pneumonia as the result of the amputation of his left arm, May 10, 1863 at Guinea Station, VA.

[5]Bosbyshell, p. 60–64.

Once again, the captain provided a colorful account of the actions around Kelly's Ford from the rest of the regiment's perspective.

[6]Bates, Vol. II. p. 13.

Hartranft, John, Staff, 51st PA, Mustered in, July 21, 1861, for 3 years, as Colonel; promoted June 8, 1864 to Brigadier General; promoted March 25, 1865 to Brevet Major General.

[7]Warner, *Generals in Blue,* p. 376–377.

Pope, John, Born March 16, 1822, in Louisville, KY; graduated from West Point in 1842; breveted to lieutenant then captain for bravery during the Mexican War; permanently promoted to captain in 1856; appointed brigadier general of volunteers on June 14, 1861; March through April 1862 successfully defeated the Confederates at Madris and Island Number 10 on the Mississippi River; promoted to major general on March

22, 1862; June 1862, given command of the Federal forces in the East which became the Army of Virginia; mishandled the Second Manassas Campaign in August 1862; transferred to the Department of the Northwest following this last campaign; died September 23, 1892.

[8]Bosbyshell. p. 61.

According to Captain Bosbyshell, the Rebel cavalry wounded a man in the 6th New Hampshire. K Company relieved B Company for the night.

[9]Warner, *Generals in Blue,* p. 447–448.

Sigel, Franz, Born November 18, 1824 in Sinseim, Baden, Germany; graduated from the Academy at Karlshrue in 1843; subaltern under Grand Duke Leopold; 1848 minister of war for the revolutionists; by 1852 had fled, respectively to Switzerland, England, and New York; 1852–1861 taught school in New York and St. Louis and was a major in 5th NY Militia; 1861 director of schools in St. Louis, MO; August 7, 1861 appointed a brigadier general; promoted March 22, 1862 to major general; saw action at Carthage, MO, Elkhorn Tavern, and Second Manassas; 1864 C.O. of the Department of West Virginia and at New Market, VA. was defeated by the cadets of Virginia Military Institute; removed from duty; resigned May 4, 1865; died August 21, 1902.

[10]Bates, Vol. I, p. 1209.

Gould, p. 408, 407.

Divine, Michael, B Co., 48th PA, Mustered in, September 19, 1861, for 3 years, as Private; killed at Fredericksburg, VA, December 13, 1862.

[11]Bates, Vol I, p. 1209–1211.

Gould, p. 409.

Brooks, Joseph, B Co., 48th Pa, Mustered in, September 19, 1861, for 3 years, as Private; mustered out., September 30, 1864—expiration of term.

Littlehales, Thomas C., B Co., 48th PA, Mustered in, September 19, 1861, for 3 years, as Private; sick in hospital, November 16, 1862; not on muster out roll.

Ward, William H., B Co., 48th PA, Mustered in, September 19, 1861, for 3 years, as Private; mustered out with Company. July 17. 1865—veteran.

Copeland, Henry, B Co., 48th PA, Mustered in, September 19, 1861, for 3 years, as private; wounded at Bull Run, VA. August 29, 1862; not on muster out roll.

Homer, John, C Co., 48th PA, Mustered in, September 19, 1861, for 3 years, as Sergeant; wounded in action, April 1, 1865; died of wounds, April 2, 1865; buried in IX Corps Cemetery, Meade Station, VA—veteran.

Kissinger, William, B Co., 48th PA, Mustered in, September 19, 1861, for 3 years, as Private; promoted to Sergeant by August 27, 1862; wounded in action, May 12, 1864; died of wounds, May 24, 1865—veteran.

[12]*Ibid.*, p. 1209–1211.

Sefrin, Joseph, B Co., 48th PA, Mustered in, September 19, 1861, for 3 years, as Private; mustered out, September 30, 1864—expiration of term.

Carlen, Philip, B Co., 48th PA, Mustered in, September 19, 1861, for 3 years, as Private; mustered out, September 30, 1864—expiration of term.

Shiterhour, Nicolas, B Co., 48th PA, Mustered in, September 19, 1861, for 3 years; died January 13, 1863; buried in Military Asylum Cemetery, Washington. DC.

[13]*Ibid.*, p. 1203.

Bertolette, John D., Staff, 48th PA, Mustered in, October 1, 1861, for 3 years, as Adjutant; promoted September 25, 1862 to Captain and Assistant Adjutant General.

[14]Warner, *Generals in Blue*, p. 258–259.

Kearny, Philip, Born June 2, 1815 in New York City; graduated in 1833 from Columbia University; practiced law; inherited one million dollars from his grandfather and immediately joined the army as a 2nd lieutenant in the 1st Dragoons in 1837; attended the French Cavalry School at Saumur; 1840 fought with the Chasseurs d'Afrique in Algiers; during the Mexican War, while serving as aide-de-camp with Winfield Scott, left arm was shattered and amputated; breveted major for gallantry; resigned from Army in 1851; traveled around the world; 1859 served in Napoleon III's Imperial Guard during the Italian War; appointed brigadier general in the U.S. service on August 7, 1861; given command of a New Jersey Brigade; spring of 1862, division commander in III Corps; July 4, 1862, promoted to major general; killed at Chantilly, VA. September 1, 1862.

[15]*Ibid.*, p. 378–380.

Porter, Fitz John, Born August 31, 1822, in Portsmouth, NH; graduated from West Point in 1845; breveted to captain and major for bravery in the Mexican War; 1849–1855 assistant instructor of artillery at West Point; 1857–1860 adjutant on the Utah Expedition; April 1861 commissioned colonel of the 15th U.S. Infantry; August 7, 1861 promoted to brigadier general; served in the Shenandoah Valley; during the Peninsular Campaign commanded a division in the III Corps then took over the V Corps; for his services, promoted to major general; during the move to Manassas, he was assigned to Pope's Army of Virginia; he detested Pope and openly voiced his contempt; at 2nd Manassas, he was given orders to "execute impossible movements" and was court-martialed and dismissed from the service on January 21, 1863; he was exonerated in 1879 and reinstated as a colonel in the Regulars in 1886; died, May 21, 1901.

[16]Bates, Vol. I, p. 1208 and 1209.

Gould, p. 406.

Basler, John G. W., B Co., 48th PA, Mustered in, September 19, 1861, for 3 years, as 3rd Sergeant; discharged November 16, 1862.

Bickert, Sebastian, B Co., 48th PA, Mustered in, September 19,

1861, for 3 years, as Private; promoted to Corporal, date not stated; promoted May 23, 1865 to Sergeant; mustered out with Company, July 17, 1865—veteran.

[17]Gould, p. 66–72.

Bosbyshell, p. 66–67.

Gould's account, in particular, contains two letters; one from Captain Pleasants (C Co.) and one from Captain Bosbyshell (G Co.), which add more detail to the battle. Neither one credits Wren and his company for covering the regiment's retreat.

[18]Bates, Vol. I, p. 1208–1211.

Gould, p. 409, 408.

Reece, Louis M., B Co., 48th PA, Mustered in, September 19, 1861, for 3 years, as Private; killed August 29, 1862, Bull Run, VA. [Gould, p. 73; L. M. Reece—missing.]

Johnson, Thomas, B Co., 48th PA [Gould, p. 73; Sergeant; wounded.]

Basler, John G., B Co., 48th PA [Gould, p. 73; Sergeant Bassler—wounded.]

Copeland, Henry T., B Co., 48th PA [Gould, p. 73; missing.]

Stanley, Samuel, B Co., 48th PA [Gould, p. 73; Samuel Stanley—missing.]

Williams, Thomas G., B Co., 48th PA, Mustered in, September 19, 1861, for 3 years, as Private; not on muster out roll. [Gould does not list him as a casualty.]

Hill, William, B Co., 48th PA, Mustered in, September 19, 1861, for 3 years, as Private; killed at Fredericksburg, VA, December 13, 1862. [Gould does not list him as a casualty.]

Kirby, Joseph, B Co., 48th PA [Gould does not list him as a casualty.]

Lucid, John, B Co., 48th PA, Mustered in, September 19, 1861, for 3 years, as Private; not on muster out roll. [Gould, p. 73; wounded.]

Heafling, John, B Co., 48th PA, Mustered in, September 19, 1861, for 3 years, as Private; mustered out, September 30, 1864—expiration of term. [Gould does not list him as a casualty.]

Bickert, Sebastian, B Co., 48th PA [Gould does not list him as a casualty.]

Shiterhour, Nicholas, B Co., 48th PA [Gould, p. 73; wounded.]

Hughes, Philip D., B Co., 48th PA, Mustered in, September 19, 1861, for 3 years, as Sergeant; promoted to 1st Sergeant, date not stated; mustered out, September 30, 1864—expiration of term. [Gould, p. 73; missing.]

Freshley, Jacob, B Co., 48th PA, Mustered in, September 19, 1861, for 3 years, as Corporal; mustered out, September 30, 1864—expiration of term. [Gould, p. 73; Corporal Freshley—wounded.]

Evans, John, B Co., 48th PA, Mustered in, September 19, 1861, for 3 years, as Private; deserted August 29, 1862; returned, March 22, 1864; promoted February 15, 1865 to Corporal; promoted June 3, 1865 to

Sergeant; mustered out with Company, July 17, 1865. [Gould, p. 73; missing.]

Rarig, Joseph, B Co., 48th PA, Mustered in, September 19, 1861, for 3 years, as Private; promoted to Corporal after August 29, 1862; promoted April 3, 1865 to Sergeant; mustered out with Company, July 17, 1865—veteran. [Gould, p. 73; Joseph Rahny—missing.]

Bradley, William, B Co., 48th PA, Mustered in, September 19, 1861, for 3 years, as Private; deserted August 29, 1862; returned March 24, 1864; mustered out with Company, July 17, 1865. [Gould, p. 73; missing.]

Johnson, George W., B Co., 48th PA, Mustered in, September 19, 1861, for 3 years, as Drummer; mustered out with Company, July 17, 1865—veteran. [Gould does not list him as a casualty.]

Evans, George, B Co., 48th PA, Mustered in, September 19, 1861, for 3 years, as Private; promoted to Corporal by August 29, 1862; mustered out September 30, 1864—expiration of term. [Gould does not list him as a casualty.]

Gould, p. 72.

Citing James Nagle's Brigade report, Gould stated that the regiment lost 7 killed; 71 wounded; 10 prisoners; 74 missing; total 152—heavy losses for a single day's action.

It is interesting to note that among those not included in Gould's list of casualties were four men hit with spent balls who were not "severely" wounded.

[19]Warner, *Generals in Blue,* p. 475–476.

Stevens, Isaac Ingalls, Born on March 25, 1818 in Andover, MA; graduated from West Point in 1839; wounded then brevetted captain and major during the Mexican War; resigned in 1853; governor of Washington Territory; July 30, 1861 appointed colonel of the 79th NY; September 28, 1861 promoted to brigadier general; served in South Carolina; July, 1862, returned to Virginia; commanded a IX Corps division at 2nd Manassas; killed September 1, 1862 at Chantilly, VA.

[20]Bates, Vol. I, p. 1208.

Major, Nelson, W., B Co., 48th PA, Mustered in, September 19, 1861, for 3 years, as Sergeant; not on muster out roll.

[21]Bates, Vol. IV, p. 189.

Wren, William, Jr., B Co., 129th PA, Mustered in, August 11, 1862, for 9 months, as Captain; mustered out with Company, May 18, 1863.

Coho, Martin V. B., B Co., 129th PA, Mustered in, August 11, 1862, for 9 months, as 1st Lieutenant; mustered out with Company, May 18, 1863.

Bosbyshell, p. 71

Bosbyshell stated that the reunion also included the 129th's adjutant, the regimental quartermaster, and one other lieutenant.

Chapter 3
Maryland

[1]Bates, Vol. I, p. 1217 and 1219.

Kleckner, Abraham, E Co., 48th PA, Mustered in, March 4, 1862, for 3 years, as Private; not on muster out roll. [Gould, p. 73; Abraham Kleckner—wounded at 2nd Manassas.]

Winlack, William, E Co., 48th PA, Mustered in, October 1, 1861, for 3 years, as Captain; mustered out, September 30, 1864—expiration of term.

[2]*Ibid.*, p. 1209 and 1210.

Gould, p. 407, 410.

Hume, Matthew, B Co., 48th PA, Mustered in, September 21, 1861, for 3 years, as Private; killed, May 12, 1864 at Spotsylvania Court House, VA.

Burk, Dominick, B Co., 48th PA, Mustered in, September 19, 1861, for 3 years, as Private; in hospital, Washington, DC, September 9, 1862; not on muster out roll.

Barnhart, John S., B Co., 48th PA, Mustered in, September 19, 1861, for 3 years, as Private; died March 8, 1864; buried at Knoxville, TN, grave Number 85.

Taylor, Thomas, B Co., 48th PA. Mustered in, September 19, 1861, for 3 years, as Private; discharged December 9, 1862, Baltimore, MD; not on muster out roll.

Harris, William, B Co., 48th PA, Mustered in, September 19, 1861, for 3 years, as Private; not on muster out roll.

[3]Warner, *Generals in Blue*, p. 486–487.

Sturgis, Samuel Davis, Born on June 11, 1822, in Shippensburg, PA; graduated West Point in 1846; lieutenant of dragoons during Mexican War and was a P.O.W. for 8 days; later served in the West as a lieutenant then a captain; April 1861 was C.O. at Fort Smith, Arkansas; escaped with most of the 1st Cavalry to Fort Leavenworth, Kansas; promoted to major; served at Wilson's Creek; March 1862, promoted to brigadier general; served at Second Manassas and Antietam as a division commander; served in the Western theater with the IX Corps; June 1864 routed at Brice's Crossroads, MS; brevetted brigadier then major general in the Regulars in March 1865; mustered out by the volunteers and became colonel of the 6th Cavalry; May 6, 1869 became colonel of the 7th Cavalry; retired in 1886 because of his age; died September 28, 1889.

[4]Bates, Vol. I. p. 1209.

Davidson, William, B Co., 48th PA, Mustered in, September 19, 1861, for 3 years, as Private; mustered out, September 30, 1864—expiration of term.

[5]*Ibid.*, p. 1209.

Eiler, Israel, B Co., 48th PA, Mustered in, September 19, 1861, for 3 years, as Private; died July 29, 1862.

[6]*Ibid.*, p. 1209.

Gould, p. 408.

Forrer, Abraham, B Co., 48th PA, Mustered in, September 19, 1861, for 3 years, as Private; died August 7, 1862.

[7]Robert U. Johnson and Clarence C. Buel, *Battles and Leaders of the Civil War*, Vol. II, The Century Co., NY, 1884, p. 600.

Edwards was part of the unattached troops assigned to the IX Corps.

Heitman, p. 398.

Edwards, Jr., John, Graduated from West Point, 1847; brevetted to 2nd Lieutenant in the 3rd Artillery on July 1, 1851; promoted to 2nd Lieutenant on March 16, 1852; promoted to 1st Lieutenant February 15, 1855; promoted to Captain on July 23, 1861; brevetted to major June 27, 1862 for gallantry; promoted to Lieutenant Colonel on September 17, 1862 for gallantry at Antietam; unassigned duty on August 11, 1871; resigned at his own request on November 7, 1870; died on October 12, 1881.

[8]Bosbyshell, p. 74–76.

Edward O. Lord, *History of the Ninth Regiment New Hampshire Volunteers in the War of the Rebellion,* Republican Press Association, Concord, NH, 1895, p. 71–87.

Both accounts paint a very glorious picture of the parts played by both of their regiments. The author of the 9th New Hampshire made it appear, as did every regiment that day, that the struggle for Fox's Gap was won by itself, exclusive of every other regiment.

James Wren Papers, Civil War Diaries, USAMHI, p. 1011–1015.

Wren mentioned in his unpublished addresses that First Lieutenant George Gowen (C Co.) volunteered to help Wren the second time his skirmish line went out but that Wren told him that one captain was enough to risk on the occasion.

[9]Bates, Vol. I, p. 1209 and 1210.

Gould, p. 409.

Bradley, Alfred E., B Co., 48th PA, Enlisted, September 19, 1861, for 3 years, as Private; mustered out with Company, July 17, 1865—veteran.

Howells, John, B Co., 48th PA, Enlisted, September 19, 1861, for 3 years, as Private; mustered out, September 30, 1864—expiration of term.

Leffler, Johnathan C., B Co., 48th PA, Enlisted, September 19, 1861; discharged, October 24, 1862, order War Department, No. 154.

Gould, p. 89–90.

He did not record any losses for B Company at South Mountain. The regiment lost 11 wounded and 1 missing for a total of 12 casualties.

[10]Bates, Vol. I, p. 1212.

Fitzpatrick, William, C Co., 48th PA, Mustered in, September 11,

1861, for 3 years, as Private; mustered out with Company, July 17, 1865—veteran.

[11]Warner, *Generals in Blue,* p. 233–235.

Hooker, Joseph, Born on November 13, 1814, in Hadley, MA; graduated from West Point in 1837; during the Mexican War rose from first lieutenant to brevet lieutenant colonel for bravery and meritorious conduct; appointed captain of 1st Artillery on October 29, 1848 but did not accept it; resigned from the Army on February 21, 1853; on August 6, 1862 he was appointed brigadier general of volunteers; demonstrated solid leadership abilities during the Peninsular, 2nd Manassas, Sharpsburg, and Fredericksburg Campaigns; Spring of 1863 promoted to command of the Army of the Potomac; lost the Battle of Chancellorsville in May, 1863; replaced as commander of the Army of the Potomac by George Meade on June 30, 1863; commanded the XX Corps at Lookout Mountain, TN, in November 1863; he resigned shortly thereafter; died October 31, 1879.

[12]Bates, Vol. III, p. 390.

Martin, Lewis J., Staff, 96th PA, Mustered in, September 23, 1861, for 3 years, as Major; killed, September 14, 1862, Crampton's Gap, MD.

[13]J. R. Sypher, comp., *History of the Pennsylvania Reserve Corps,* Elias Barr and Co., Lancaster, PA, 1865, p. 604.

Shoemaker, Jacob W., Lieutenant, F Co., 4th PA Res., 33rd Regt. PA Vols.; captured at 2nd Bull Run, VA; promoted to Captain.

[14]Bates, Vol. I, p. 1208.

Davis, David J., B Co., 48th PA, Mustered in, September 19, 1861, for 3 years, as Corporal; killed May 12, 1864 at Spotsylvania Court House, VA—veteran.

James Wren Papers, Civil War Diaries, USAMHI, p. 721.

After the war, Wren paid the tough little Scot the following tribute. "... Dye Davis whips and slashes the whole company when in Liquor. And I ordered him to be tied on a plank with roaps [ropes] in the guard house until he got sober and after he was on the plank and became somewhat sobered up, he said he wanted to see the captain. [I said], 'Tell him I can't be bothered with him' and I did not go to see him [at] the first call, and he begged on the sergeant to just get the Captain to come. I went to see him, 'Well, Dye, what do [you] want with me?' [Dye] 'I do want you to take me off this plank.' 'No, sir, I will not take you off. You told me before that you would keep sober and be a man. There's no man in you.' And he commenced to be [a man] and [he] said, 'O What would my Meary [Mary] say if she saw me hear?' [Wren:] 'What would your Mary—your Mary would be just like me. When she married you, she thought she had a man and when I enlisted [you] I thought I had a man, but we ware both mistaken.' and he burst into tears and said, 'O, Captain, do take me off hear, and [I] will show you I will be a man.' [Wren:] 'I know you can be a man if you try,' and with this promise he was released and he gave me his word he would be a man hearafter and he kept his word and a braver and better soldier then Dye Davis was not in the service; he was wounded 3 times, but, alas, the fatal shot he received at the Wilderness, but his Mary was the great coard to be touched."

[15]Lillian Henderson, comp., *Roster of the Confederate Soldiers of Georgia*, Vol. I, by mandate of the Governor, 1958, p. 394.

Holmes, William R., Captain, D Co., 4nd Georgia, April 19, 1861; elected Lieutenant Colonel April 28, 1862; killed at Sharpsburg, MD, September 17, 1862.

[16]*Ibid.*, p. 1210.

Moyer, Laurentis C., B Co., 48th PA, Mustered in, September 19, 1861, for 3 years, as Private; killed May 12, 1864 at Spotsylvania Court House, VA—veteran.

Gould, p. 90.

He listed all three as being wounded on September 17, 1862.

[17]Bates, Vol. I, p. 1209–1210.

Gould, p. 409, 408.

Robinson, John, B Co., 48th PA, Mustered in, September 19, 1861, for 3 years, as Private; killed at Antietam, MD, September 17, 1862.

Heaton, Carey, B Co., 48th PA, Mustered in, September 19, 1861, for 3 years, as Private; wounded December 13, 1862 at Fredericksburg, VA; mustered out with Company, July 17, 1865—veteran.

Gould, p. 90.

Gould included Robinson as "Robinson" among the wounded along with one John R. Simpson, who does not appear on Bates' roster.

[18]Bates, Vol. I, p. 1210.

Gould, p. 409.

Prince, Alexander, B Co., 48th PA, Mustered in, September 19, 1861, for 3 years, as Private; killed September 17, 1862 at Antietam, MD; not on muster out roll.

Bosbyshell, p. 82.

Captain Bosbyshell mistakenly referred to Prince as a sergeant. He added that Prince, while offering the wounded man water, was shot and that the captain could still hear the private's death cry as the bullet plucked him off his feet.

Gould, p. 90.

The regiment lost 8 killed and 51 wounded for a total of 59 casualties.

[19]Bates, Vol. I, p. 1208 and 1209.

Watkins, John, B Co., 48th PA, Mustered in, September 19, 1861, for 3 years, as Private; promoted May 22, 1865 to 2nd Lieutenant; mustered out with Company, July 17, 1865—veteran.

Colihan, John, B Co., 48th PA, Mustered in, September 19, 1861, for 3 years, as Private; mustered out, September 30, 1864—expiration of term.

[20]Microfilm Roster at USAMHI, card 5–1162.

Cathers, John, H Co., 6th Infantry Militia, 1862, Enrolled, September 12, 1862, at St. Clair, Schuylkill County, PA; mustered in as Private; age 31; height 5'9"; sandy complexion; occupation, machinist; brown hair; discharged September 27, 1862.

[21]Bates, Vol. I, p. 1220.

Williams, John L., F Co., 48th PA, Mustered in, October 1, 1861, for 3 years, as 2nd Lieutenant; promoted July 13, 1864 to 1st Lieutenant; promoted October 30, 1864 to Captain; mustered out with Company, July 17, 1865—veteran.

[22]*Ibid.*, p. 1223.

Jackson, Henry C., G Co., 48th PA, Mustered in, October 1, 1861, for 3 years, as 1st Sergeant; promoted June 2, 1862 to 2nd Lieutenant; killed in action, May 12, 1864, Spotsylvania Court House—buried in National Cemetery near Fredericksburg.

[23]*Ibid.*, p. 1217.

Bohannon, Thomas, E Co., 48th PA, Mustered in, October 1, 1861, for 3 years, as 2nd Lieutenant; promoted September 17, 1862 as 1st Lieutenant; promoted June 23, 1865 to Regimental Quartermaster; mustered out with Regiment, July 17, 1865.

[24]*Ibid.*, p. 1226.

Hinkle, William J., H Co., 48th PA, Mustered in, September 19, 1861, for 3 years, as 1st Lieutenant; promoted August 28, 1863 to Captain; commissioned but not mustered, January 2, 1865 to Major; mustered out, March 5, 1865—expiration of term.

[25]*Ibid.*, p. 1203.

Ellis, James, Staff, 48th PA, Mustered in October 1, 1861, for 3 years, as Regimental Quartermaster; resigned December 20, 1862.

Chapter 4
Virginia Again

[1]Warner, *Generals in Blue*, p. 373–374.

Pleasonton, Alfred, Born on July 7, 1824, in Washington, DC; graduated from West Point in 1844; brevetted to 1st lieutenant for bravery in the Mexican War; served in the West against the Indians and in the Seminole War; commanded the 2nd Dragoons in the Utah Expedition; promoted February 15, 1862 to major; served in the Peninsular Campaign; promoted to brigadier general on July 18, 1862; division commander of the Cavalry Corps during the Maryland Campaign, Fredericksburg, and

Chancellorsville; promoted to major general on June 22, 1863; by then he was commander of the Cavalry Corps; relieved of command by U.S. Grant on March 25, 1864; served in the Department of the Missouri for the balance of the war; died, February 17, 1897.

[2]*Ibid.*, p. 558–559.

Willcox, Orlando Bolivar, Born on April 16, 1823, in Detroit, MI; graduated from West Point in 1847; resigned in 1857; practiced law until 1861; 1861, colonel of 1st Michigan Infantry; wounded and captured at 1st Manassas; P.O.W. for one year; August 19, 1862, released and commissioned to brigadier general; led the 1st Division and sometimes the IX Corps during the Maryland Campaign, Fredericksburg, Knoxville and the Overland Campaign; held his division command until the end of the war; served in the West on staff level until his retirement in 1887; died, May 10, 1907, age 84.

[3]Bates, Vol, I, p. 1217.

Nagle, Abraham, D Co., 48th PA, Mustered in, September 23, 1861, for 3 years, as Private; not on muster out roll.

[4]Warner, *Generals in Blue,* p. 361–362.

Patrick, Marsena Rudolph, Born on March 11, 1811, near Watertown, NY; graduated from West Point in 1835; spent 5 years in the 2nd Infantry in Mexico and the Seminole War; brevetted to major as chief of commissary under General Wool; resigned in 1850 to farm in Geneva, NY; April 1861 became inspector general for NY; March 20, 1862 commissioned a brigadier general; brigade commander at 2nd Manassas, South Mountain, and Antietam; became provost marshal general until the end of the war; March 13, 1865 brevetted to major general; died July 27, 1888.

[5]Bates, Vol. IV. p. 185.

Frick, Jacob, Staff, 129th PA, Mustered in August 15, 1862, for 9 months, as Colonel; mustered out with regiment, May 18, 1863.

[6]*Ibid.*, p. 189.

Parvin, Jacob, Jr., B Co., 129th PA, Mustered in, August 11, 1862, for 9 months, as 2nd Lieutenant; wounded in action, December 13, 1862 at Fredericksburg, VA; died of wounds, December 14, 1862.

[7]Bosbyshell, p. 96–101.

Gould, p. 94–108.

Gould included several letters from participants which add a little extra perspective to the regiment's role in the engagement.

[8]Warner, *Generals in Blue,* p. 159–160 and 489–490.

Sumner, Edwin Vose, Born on January 30, 1797, in Boston, MA; commissioned into the U.S. Army in 1819; nicknamed "Bull Head"; captain of dragoons in 1833; major of dragoons in 1846; brevetted to lieutenant colonel, then colonel in the Mexican War; 1848 commissioned as a lieutenant colonel; 1855 became colonel of the 1st Cavalry; 1861 promoted to brigadier general in the Regular army; C.O. of the II Corps during the Peninsular Campaign; wounded twice during that campaign; promoted to major general on July 16, 1862; served at Antietam and at Fredericksburg; died March 21, 1863.

Franklin, William Buel, Born of February 27, 1823 at York, PA; graduated from West Point in 1843; commissioned in the Corps of Topographical Engineers from 1843–1845; served under Kearny in the Rockies; brevetted for bravery during the Mexican War; stationed in Washington, DC until 1861; May 14, 1861 was commissioned colonel of the 12th U.S. Infantry; May 17, 1861 was promoted to brigadier general; led a division then the VI Corps during the Peninsular Campaign; commanded the Corps through the 2nd Manassas Campaign; the Antietam Campaign, in which his men took Crampton's Gap from the Confederates; at Fredericksburg, he commanded the "Left Grand Division"; Burnside criticized his efforts and demanded he resign from the service; given the command of the XIX Corps at Sabine Pass and Red River, TX; died on March 8, 1903.

[9]Pollock Letters, USAMHI.
Letter to Mother, December 18, 1862.
He wrote to his mother about the chimney falling incidents.

"...About four o'clock we were marched down the street nearest the river to about the middle of the town and halted just in front of where a whole block house had been burned to the ground, nothing was left of them, but the tall chimneys fell down with a loud crash and as the men were lying all around under them at every little [space] there was, we all supposed two or three must be badly injured, if not killed, but by good fortune, all the men got out but one, who was not seriously injured, he being near the bottom..." [Gould, p. 103. That man was one of five injured in E Company.]

"...I do not know how long I slept, but I awoke feeling very cold, and hearing a great deal of commotion around I got up and saw a crowd around one of the fires, and on asking what it meant, learned that another chimney had falled down and hurt another man. I jumped up and went over. The doctor was there and I could tell by his face that he was seriously injured. He was carried off to the hospital but died before morning."

[10]*Massachusetts Soldiers, Sailors, and Marines*, Vol. II. p. 596.
Clark, William S., Staff, 21st MA, age 35; commissioned and mustered August 23, 1861 as Major; mustered and commissioned February 28, 1862 as Lieutenant Colonel; mustered and commissioned May 16, 1862 as Colonel; resigned and discharged April 22, 1863.

[11]Bosbyshell, p. 97.
Bosbyshell, who was next to Jackson, recalled, "A shell exploded seemingly immediately in front of us, and just above our heads. He [Bosbyshell] was unharmed, save dazed by the brilliant flash—whilst Jackson's neck was pitted and marked by the powder from the shell—looking as though he had the black smallpox. Poor fellow, he was unfortunate in every engagement he was in, and finally lost his life at the battle of Spotsylvania."

[12]Bates, Vol. I, p. 1209.

Gould, p. 407.

Brown, Richard, B Co., 48th PA, Mustered in, September 19, 1861, for 3 years, as Private; wounded December 13, 1862 at Fredericksburg, VA; not on muster out roll.

[13]*Ibid.*, p. 1226.

Thompson, Alba C., H Co., 48th PA, Mustered in, September 19, 1861, for 3 years, as Corporal; promoted to Sergeant after Fredericksburg; promoted September 12, 1864 to 2nd Lieutenant; promoted October 30, 1864 to 1st Lieutenant; promoted March 3, 1865 to Captain; mustered out with Company, July 17, 1865—veteran.

[14]Gould, p. 103.

According to Gould, the 48th lost 7 killed, 43 wounded, and 1 missing for a total of 51.

[15]Warner, *Generals in Blue*, p. 515.

Tyler, Erastus Barnard, Born on April 24, 1822 in West Bloomfield, NY; in 1861 helped raise the 7th Ohio Volunteers; regiment lost its first action on August 28, 1861; commanded a brigade at Kernstown and Port Republic; promoted to brigadier general on May 14, 1862; August 1862, given a brigade in the V Corps; served at Antietam and Fredericksburg; June 30, 1863 was assigned to duty around Baltimore; mustered out in August, 1865; died, January 9, 1891.

[16]Warner, *Generals in Gray*, p. 56.

Cobb, Thomas Reade Rootes; Born April 10, 1823, at "Cherry Hill", Jefferson County, GA; graduated from University of Georgia and became a prominent lawyer; recruited Cobb's Legion in 1861 and became its colonel; served very well in the Peninsular, Second Manassas, and Maryland Campaigns; promoted, November 1, 1862 to brigadier general; wounded December 13, 1862 at Fredericksburg, VA; bled to death the same day.

[17]Bates, Vol, I, p. 1204, 1208, and 1224.

Evans, Charles B., G Co., 48th PA, Mustered in, October 1, 1861, for 3 years, as Corporal; promoted to Sergeant, date not stated; promoted September 17, 1864 to Hospital Steward; mustered out with regiment, July 17, 1865—veteran.

Stouch, Samuel C., B Co., 48th PA, Mustered in, September 19, 1861 for 3 years, as Corporal; promoted to Sergeant, date not stated; discharged on Surgeon's certificate, September, 1864.

Postscript

[1]Bates, Vol. I. p. 1203 and 1208.

[2]Wren Papers and Civil War Diary, Manuscript Dept., USAMHI.

Bibliography

Bates, Samuel P., "Forty-Eighth Regiment." *History of Pennsylvania Volunteers*, Vol. I, II, B. Singerly, State Printers, Harrisburg, PA, 1869.

Bosbyshell, Oliver C., *The 48th in the War*, Avil Printing Co., Philadelphia.

Connecticut Adjutant General's Office. *Record of Service of Connecticut Men in the Army and Navy of the United States During the War of the Rebellion.* Press of the Case, Lockwood, and Brainard Company, Hartford, CT, 1889.

Gould, Joseph, *The Story of the Forty-Eighth.* Regimental Association, 1908.

Heitman, Francis B., *Historical Register and Dictionary of the United States Army*, Vol. I, U.S. Government Printing Office, Washington, DC, 1903. (Reprint, University of Illinois, 1965.)

Henderson, Lillian, comp., *Roster of the Confederate Soldiers of Georgia 1861–1865*, Vol. I, by mandate of the Governor, 1958.

Johnson, Robert U, and Clarence C. Buel, *Battles and Leaders of the Civil War*, Vol. II, The Century Co., NY, 1884.

Jordon, Jr., Weymouth T., *North Carolina Troops 1861–1865,* Vol. IX, Division of Archives and History, Raleigh, NC.

Lord, Edward O., *History of the Ninth Regiment New Hampshire Volunteers in the War of the Rebellion,* Republican Press Association, Concord, NH, 1895.

Massachusetts' Adjutant General, *Massachusetts Soldiers, Sailors, and Marines in the Civil War*, Vol. II, Norwood Press, Norwood, MA, 1931.

Microfilm Roster at USAMHI, card 5–1162.

New York Adjutant General *Report*, 1896.

Pollock, Curtis C., Letters, Civil War Miscellaneous Collection, USAMHI.

Powell, William H. and Edward Shippen, *Officers of the Army and Navy*, L. R. Hamersly and Co., Philadelphia, PA, 1892.

Rhode Island Adjutant General's Office. *Official Roster of Rhode Island Officers and Soldiers Who Served in the United States Army and Navy. From, 1861 to 1866,* by order of the General Assembly, January Session, 1866.

Roe, Alfred S., *Twenty-Fourth Regiment Massachusetts Volunteers, 1861– 1866. "New England Guard Regiment"*, 1907.

Sypher, J. R., comp., *History of the Pennsylvania Reserve Corps*, Elias Barr and Co., Lancaster, 1865.

Thompson, Herbert S., *First Defenders,* 1910.

Warner, Ezra J., *Generals in Blue.* Louisiana State University Press, Baton Rouge, LA.

Warner, Ezra J., *Generals in Gray,* Louisiana State University Press, Baton Rouge, LA.

Wren, James, Papers, Civil War Diaries, USAMHI.

Epilogue

When we started this assignment in the autumn of 1988, my students and I had no idea the project would be published. In order to obtain funding, I contacted Bob Brown, at the Talented and Gifted Office at the Washington County Board of Education, and he processed the initial paperwork with the Maryland Humanities Council. Later he and I scheduled two visits to the United States Army Military History Institute Library in Carlisle Barracks, Pennsylvania.

I explained the proposal of editing a diary to all my freshman U.S. Studies classes, and word spread to several of my former students. More than a dozen students responded to the proposal. We agreed to meet once a week after school. During the first two meetings, I provided each student with a portion of the diary and instructed them to write down the name of every individual they could find. This tedious process eliminated the uncertain and left behind a group of ten students from the freshman, sophomore, and junior classes. I divided the ten into pairs and gave each a specific assignment.

One pair had to list as many of James Wren's peculiar spellings as possible. They soon discovered these included almost everything he wrote. Another searched the Official Record of the War of the Rebellion for accounts from the 48th Pennsylvania. A third was to look for information in *Generals in Blue* and *Generals in Gray*. The fourth looked for pictures and photographs about the regiment and its battles. The last team had to find the Official Records' maps to locate the regiment's war time itinerary.

All except one student could take the two field trips to

Carlisle. Again the students formed teams, as explained in the Introduction. The three working in the manuscript department hated leaving the room, except to eat lunch. They became involved in Wren's recollections, and Curtis Pollock's letters, and discovered a world they had never seen. When Pete Cartwright realized he was touching material dating from the Civil War period, his eyes lit up and I could not pry him out of the room. Pete discovered the captain's letter of resignation. Rob Mueller carefully recorded Curtis Pollock's letters from New Bern to Fredericksburg. He found the young officer's plea to his father, asking him to persuade the governor to secure his promotion to lieutenant. Brian Blickenstaff meticulously plodded through Wren's postwar memoirs and discovered the captain's unique sense of humor.

Another highlight of the trip occurred when Jessica Rauth and Matt Pfister discovered the very obscure Lieutenant Flagler in a second edition of a very hard to get book. They acted as if they had discovered gold. Matt is still so enthralled with the Civil War that he has seen the movie "Glory" three times. He cannot wait to take part in next year's project.

The entire experience made amateur detectives and sleuths of all of us. When White Mane offered to publish the diary, the entire research team decided to donate all of the royalties to our high school to promote further historical research. We have achieved a "first" for our school and for our country and we have all come out winners. I am so proud of these students.

This book is a hallmark, an example of what a teacher and willing students can do if they set their minds to it. Wherever possible, history should be taught through as many primary sources as possible. History is an active art form which involves individuals and their lives. It is neither static nor boring. It requires scrutiny, evaluation, interpretation, and clarification. Students who are actively engaged in the historical process will carry some of those skills into other classes and future careers.

There are many excellent research facilities within this

country which many high school students and teachers have never used. The Library of Congress, the National Archives, the U.S. Army Military History Institute Library, the Virginia Historical Society, local college and university libraries, county and town libraries, county historical societies and the library collections of our National Parks Service contain books, newspapers, magazines, and manuscripts which are there for the American public to utilize. I will never forget the sense of awe I saw in my students' faces when they walked into the book stacks at the U.S. Army Military History Institute Library. They had never seen such a collection of military books before. They were equally surprised by the holdings of the Western Maryland Room of the Washington County Library. The field trips exposed them to a fascinating new world for them to explore. It was terrific to watch them scour the shelves for materials related to their topics.

As a teacher, I am obligated to show the exciting world of learning beyond the prescribed curriculum to those who want to see it. English, writing, thinking, and genuine learning all combine into a creative process which happens to be based in history. We all learned by doing, by being involved, as the testimonials of these two participants verify.

Matt Pfister:

"The personal experience that I gained on our trips to Carlisle War College was one of an understanding of what a historian has to go through to research the people and places that create history. I remember the hours that I spent drowning in books, trying to find one meaningful fact or date, seemed to be in vain, but now that I look back on the book and see how people are important, not the fact or the date. I've learned a lot from our trips and from the little things we dug up such as some of the accounts of the emotional impact the war had on a lot of men.

"Putting the book together was a lot of fun. It also was a great learning experience to be there. It was a thrill to actually draw something and to see it published with my name on it. I look at it all now and I think it is amazing to be a part of a group of South Hagerstown High School's students, to actually be the first group of high school students to make history with a book on history."

Rob Mueller:

"Working with Mr. Priest on the diary of James Wren was an outstanding experience for me. After learning so much outside of the classroom, and actually enjoying it, maybe the school system should encourage more of these projects.

"By transcribing the letters of several Civil War soldiers, I felt like I was on a personal basis with them. In a normal history class there is no time to get personal with the people that are a part of history.

"To Mr. Priest, I offer my sincerest thanks, and I hope he becomes a standard for a teacher's interest in his students."

Index